Eighteen Years with Enya

What You Seek to Change, Changes You

Amar B. Singh

Amar B. Singh

To Enya,

*my greatest teacher,
who taught me everything by being exactly who she is;*

and

*to all the families learning
that what we seek to change,
changes us.*

Amar B. Singh

© 2025 Amar B. Singh

All rights reserved

Amar B. Singh spent the first decade of his career building expertise in strategic consulting and marketing, operating in a world where problems had solutions and effort produced predictable results. He specialized in organizational analysis, change management, and the kind of systematic thinking that corporate environments reward.

Then parenthood introduced him to challenges that couldn't be strategized away.

When his daughter Enya was diagnosed with autism, Amar discovered that all his professional skills – planning, analysis, problem-solving – not only failed to help but often made things worse. This collision between his expertise and reality sparked a fundamental questioning that led to entirely new frameworks for understanding resilience, intelligence, and human potential.

Over eighteen years of learning from Enya's unique way of being, Singh developed what he calls the "Delta Mind" philosophy and the "Odyssey Equation" – practical frameworks for navigating life's uncontrollable challenges. These aren't theoretical constructs but lived discoveries, forged through daily experience with someone whose consciousness operates according to principles that conventional psychology doesn't recognize.

For the past fifteen years, Amar has worked with hundreds of people dealing with circumstances that resist traditional intervention approaches. His role isn't to provide solutions but to support the kind of awareness shifts that allow individuals and families to move from exhausting attempts at control towards recognition of unexpected forms of wisdom.

This work grew organically from his own transformation. As his ambition for conventional success naturally dissolved, it was replaced by an overwhelming desire to share what he had learned – not through teaching in any formal sense, but through offering his experience to others navigating similar territories.

Amar's previous books have focused on several topics including philosophy, relationships, spirituality, business strategy and socio-economic effects of technology. This memoir represents his most personal work – a detailed account of discovering that some of the most sophisticated forms of human intelligence operate outside the frameworks our institutions are designed to recognize or support but have a huge transformation potential for us.

He approaches this subject not as an autism expert or special needs authority, but as someone who underwent a complete reversal of understanding about who was teaching whom. His perspective is that of a student sharing discoveries that continue to unfold, a fellow traveler offering maps of territory he's still exploring.

Amar lives in India with his family, where he continues his daily education in presence, authenticity, and the many forms that consciousness can take. He remains actively involved in supporting individuals and families with the recognition of human differences as nature's gift to us.

His work integrates insights from multiple wisdom traditions including Hindu philosophy, consciousness studies, technology, and systems thinking, coupled with his practical experience around supporting people through some of life's most challenging circumstances. This polymathic approach reflects his conviction that the most important human challenges require perspectives that transcend any single discipline or methodology.

Through his writing, consulting, and community building, Amar advocates for a fundamental shift from asking "How can we help different people become more "normal"?" to "What can different ways of being human teach us about consciousness, intelligence, and authentic living?"

"Eighteen Years with Enya" represents the culmination of his most important learning and the foundation for everything he now understands about resilience, awareness, and the unexpected sources from which wisdom emerges. Although his first book was *"A Week With Enya"*, this is his first memoir and the most honest account he can offer of an education that required no enrollment but transformed everything he thought he knew about what makes a life meaningful.

When not writing or working in his role as a growth leader, Amar practices the daily discipline that Enya taught him: learning to see the extraordinary intelligence that operates through even the most ordinary appearances, and receiving the teachings that life offers through every encounter with what we don't yet understand.

Preface

As Enya turns eighteen, I realize I had been documenting the journey of helping my autistic daughter navigate our world. I never expected to discover I was actually recording my apprenticeship with a teacher I'd been too busy trying to fix to notice.

This memoir chronicles eighteen years of learning from Enya, who has never spoken a full sentence yet taught me everything about presence, authenticity, and consciousness itself.

It began as every autism story does – with diagnosis and desperate searches for answers. It evolved into something unexpected: a spiritual education disguised as special needs parenting.

What This Journey Became

When Enya was diagnosed at two, I thought I knew our path: therapists, interventions, helping her adapt to society's expectations. I never imagined the journey would become one of learning to see our world through her eyes.

Around her eighth birthday, during a week I spent alone with her, a question cracked everything open: What if she wasn't the one who needed to change?

The book includes a few poems from my first book *A Week With Enya*, to hopefully, bring in the genuine flavor of the emergence of my understanding.

What This Book Offers

This is the story of eighteen years walking alongside someone who embodies what mystics spend lifetimes seeking. You'll find therapy sessions and breakthrough moments, meltdowns and quiet victories – the ordinary magic of raising any child and the extraordinary teachers that emerge when you stop trying to normalize what might already be perfect.

This isn't another clinical guide to autism. Excellent practical resources exist elsewhere. This book serves a different purpose: exploring what happens when we ask different questions.

Traditional autism literature asks: How can we help these children fit into our world?

This book asks: What if their silence isn't absence but presence so complete it doesn't need words? What if their repetitive behaviors aren't compulsions but meditation practices? What if the children we call "special" are demonstrating forms to try of consciousness our world has forgotten how to recognize?

Who This Is For

If you're exhausted by books that reduce your child to deficits and delays, if you've sensed there's more to their story than clinical reports capture, if you're ready to question everything you think you know about intelligence and consciousness – then perhaps we can explore this territory together.

This book is for parents who love fiercely but suspect their child might be carrying wisdom they haven't learned to recognize. It's for anyone wondering whether the differences we pathologize might be expressions of consciousness operating from entirely different principles.

The Invitation

Every parent faces a choice: remain in frameworks that see only deficits to repair, or step into the mystery that asks whether your child might embody exactly the consciousness our world needs.

The choice doesn't determine your child's nature – that remains constant. But it determines everything about how you'll experience the extraordinary privilege of learning from them.

Come. Let me tell you about my daughter, my teacher, my guide into the language of being that exists beyond words.

Let me tell you about eighteen years with Enya.

Contents

Preface	8
Prologue	13
PART I: THE SLEEPING YEARS	15
1. The First Silence	16
2. The Day the Family Cried	29
3. Therapies and Thresholds	36
PART II: THE AWAKENING	56
Clueless Years	57
4. A Week with Enya - The Electric Shock	59
What you seek to change, changes you!	66
5. The Hand That Knows	69
The Deep Lake	84
6. Intelligence in Disguise	87
The Pursuit of Intelligence	103
PART III: THE DEEPENING	105
Seizure	106
7. The Seizure – Dense Helplessness	108
How Many Deaths Can One Die!	115
8. The All- Knowing Glance	119
9. Love Without Language: Her Universe, Her Rules	138
10. The Wave Realizes the Ocean	154
The Leaf is the Tree	161

Epilogue: From Wave to Ocean 165
Acknowledgments 172
   Glossary 177
   Appendix A: The Three-Level Consciousness Framework 181

Prologue

I write these words last – during Durga Puja – one month before Enya turns eighteen.

The *dhol* beats echo from the *pandals* nearby, celebrating the Goddess whose name she bears. Ananya – one of Durga's many names – sits beside me with the kind of focused awareness that most people never bring to anything.

She doesn't speak, hasn't spoken a meaningful sentence in eighteen years. But in that quality of presence, I recognize something that took me nearly two decades to see: she has been my greatest teacher.

Not the inspirational teacher of well-meaning platitudes, but a literal teacher offering lessons I didn't know I needed. For most of her life, I believed I was helping her navigate our world. I measured success by her progress toward conventional milestones, evaluated our relationship by how well I was preparing her for what I assumed would constitute fulfillment.

I had it completely wrong.

She looks up at me now with that expression I've learned to recognize – not seeking anything, just offering the gift of complete presence. In that glance, I see eighteen years of teachings that gradually wore away my certainty about who was helping whom.

This is the story of an apprenticeship I didn't know I was enrolled in – how someone I thought needed guidance was actually guiding me toward forms of awareness I had never imagined possible.

The festival drums remind me that divinity is usually celebrated with noise and ceremony. But here sits a different kind of divine – one that needs no festival, no fanfare. Her presence is her celebration.

Forty days from now, we light eighteen candles. The world will call it her passage to adulthood. I know better now. The real passage has been mine – from sleeping awareness to recognition of what she came to teach.

This is the story of that awakening.

PART I: THE SLEEPING YEARS

1. The First Silence

In the beginning was connection,

and I celebrated what I thought

would last forever,

never knowing I was witnessing

both hello and goodbye.

She arrived on Monday midnight, in November at Jamshedpur, when the first hints of winter touched the air. The cesarean delivery was smooth, the doctors declared her healthy, and a nurse came out holding my daughter. I smiled with the relief that follows nine months of anticipation.

"She's so quiet," the nurse commented, adjusting the blanket around her. "Most babies cry more in the first few hours."

At the time, I took this as a blessing. A quiet baby meant easier nights, didn't it? Less disruption to the carefully constructed life my wife and I had built.

The first year unfolded like a love story. Enya was everything I had hoped for in a daughter – responsive, engaging, delightfully interactive. She would lock eyes with me during our morning routines, her face lighting up with recognition when I appeared in front of her. When I made silly faces or played peek-a-boo, she would reward me with smiles that felt like pure sunshine.

She babbled in that musical way that babies do, carrying on elaborate conversations in her own language while maintaining perfect eye contact. I would respond seriously to her babbling, and she would babble back, as if we were discussing the most important matters in the world.

"Look at her watching you," my wife would say during our evening play sessions. "She never takes her eyes off you when you're playing."

This was true. Enya had developed what I thought of as laser-focus attention when we were engaged together. She would study my face intently when I sang to her, reach for toys I offered, laugh at the right moments during our games. She seemed genuinely interested in the world we were showing her.

But even then, there were subtle signs that I would only recognize in retrospect. She was less interested in strangers than other babies seemed to be. While she would light up for family members, she would often turn away when visitors tried to engage her. I attributed this to natural shyness or stranger anxiety – perfectly normal developmental phases that all babies go through.

"She's just selective," I would tell concerned relatives who noticed her lack of response to their attempts at interaction. "She knows who her people are."

The pediatric checkups during her first year were reassuring. She was meeting her physical milestones beautifully – sitting up, crawling, pulling herself to standing. Her motor development was actually ahead of schedule in some areas. The doctor was pleased with her progress.

One of the earliest signs of her cognitive abilities was when the moment she would enter the hospital premises for vaccinations. Her little face would get slightly serious and at the sight of the doctor she would start crying out aloud. We told the doctor, "she recognizes you and somehow knows she's going to feel the pain of an injection."

"She's a bright one," he would say, watching her watch him during examinations. "Look how focused she is."

***

Her first birthday celebration in Jamshedpur was magical. Surrounded by extended family, she seemed happy and engaged, though in her own quiet way. She was walking by then, exploring the house with careful determination. She would take my hand and lead me to things she found interesting – a particular texture on the wall, sunlight streaming through a window, the dog on the street.

"She's such a calm child," my mother observed. "Not like these other one-year-olds who are running around creating chaos."

I was proud of this assessment. We had somehow been blessed with a child who was both engaged and manageable, bright but not overwhelming. She seemed perfect to me – exactly what I had imagined parenthood would be like.

But then came the vaccination appointment at fifteen months.

***

The MMR shot was routine – a standard part of the immunization schedule that millions of children receive without incident. The pediatrician administered it efficiently while I held Enya steady. She cried briefly, as most children do, then settled down as we prepared to leave.

"She might be a little fussy for a day or two," the doctor mentioned casually. "Some children run a low fever or feel tired after this one."

I expected crankiness, maybe some disrupted sleep. I never expected what actually happened.

Within days – maybe a week – it was as if someone had replaced my daughter with a different child. The transformation wasn't gradual; it was sudden and complete, like a light switching off.

The eye contact that had been the foundation of all our interactions simply disappeared. When I tried to catch her gaze during our usual play sessions, she would look through me, past me, anywhere but at my face. The baby who had always looked at me directly during conversations was now staring at the ceiling, the walls, her own hands – anything except the people who loved her.

Her babbling stopped almost entirely. The musical conversations we had enjoyed were replaced by silence broken only by occasional sounds that seemed directed at objects rather than people. She no longer responded when I called her name, no longer turned toward my voice with that expectant smile.

Most alarming was her sudden fascination with textures and repetitive movements. She would spend hours running her fingers along the corner of her pillow, tracing the seam with an intensity that seemed to shut out the entire world. She discovered that she could pull her hair up at the top of her head and tug at the strands while her eyes moved inward toward her nose, holding this position for long periods as if finding some necessary relief in the sensation.

"She's been like this for two hours," my wife said one afternoon, watching Enya examine pillow corners with unwavering focus. "I've called her name twenty times. She won't look up."

I tried to convince myself this was temporary – a phase that would pass once the vaccination effects wore off. But days turned into weeks, and the engaging child I had known seemed to have retreated somewhere I couldn't reach.

The baby who had once studied my face with devoted attention now seemed more interested in the patterns light made on the wall. The child who had laughed at my silly games now found her entertainment in repetitive movements that I couldn't understand or interrupt without causing distress.

"Maybe she's just going through a developmental leap," I suggested to my wife, grasping for explanations that would make this transformation temporary and manageable.

But privately, I was beginning to feel the first stirrings of panic. This wasn't the typical regression that some children experience during growth spurts. This felt like losing her – not physically, but losing access to the connection we had built during her first fifteen months of life.

The child who had once reached for me when she saw me coming now barely seemed to register my presence. The baby who had laughed and babbled responsively in our mock conversations had fallen into a silence that felt both profound and impenetrable.

I found myself grieving for the daughter I had known while trying to understand the daughter I was now living with. She was still beautiful, still mine, still the same physical child. But the connection that had defined our relationship – the eye contact, the responsive interactions, the sense of mutual delight in each other's presence – had vanished as suddenly as if someone had flipped a switch.

The transformation was so complete and so sudden that I couldn't help wondering what had changed. The timing felt too coincidental to ignore. The child I had known for fifteen months had disappeared shortly after that routine medical appointment, replaced by someone who seemed to inhabit a completely different reality.

But questions about causation felt less important than the immediate challenge of learning how to connect with this new version of my daughter. The engaging baby was gone, and in her place was a child who seemed to have travelled somewhere I couldn't follow – a place where pillow corners were more interesting than faces, where repetitive movements brought more satisfaction than interactive play.

I didn't yet know that this would be the beginning of an eighteen-year journey of learning to see intelligence and connection in forms I had never imagined. I didn't understand that losing the child I thought I knew would eventually lead me to discover a teacher I never expected.

All I knew was that the daughter who had once looked into my eyes with such focused attention was now looking everywhere else, and I had no idea how to find my way back to her – or if the path back even existed.

A Diagnosis and a Doorway

The months following Enya's transformation settled into a new normal that I kept expecting to be temporary. She remained the calm, physically capable child she had always been, but the interactive spark that had defined her first fifteen months seemed to have relocated somewhere I couldn't access.

She would still take my hand sometimes and lead me to things that interested her, but these were different kinds of interests now – textures, patterns, repetitive sensations rather than shared discoveries. She had developed an elaborate morning ritual of examining her bedsheet, running her fingers along the fabric for thirty minutes or more, completely absorbed in whatever information she was gathering from the repetitive motion.

Her focus had become both more intense and more selective. While she had once divided her attention between objects and people, she now seemed to find far more fascination in inanimate things than in human interactions. The pillow corner examination could last for hours if uninterrupted.

I told myself this was normal development, that children go through phases of intense focus and absorption. But the lack of eye contact continued to trouble me in ways I couldn't articulate. The child who had once studied my face with such devoted attention now looked everywhere except at the people who loved her.

By eighteen months, these changes had become impossible to ignore or explain away as temporary phases.

***

We were visiting my parents in Jamshedpur, six months after her transformation, when the full reality of the situation became undeniable. The house was full of relatives gathered for a family celebration, and the contrast between Enya and the other children her age was stark.

My sister's daughter, just a few months younger than Enya, was running around the house chattering constantly, engaging with every adult who paid attention to her, responding immediately when her name was called. She would look directly at people when they spoke to her, answer questions with enthusiastic babbling, seek out interaction and connection.

Enya, by contrast, seemed to exist in a separate reality. She had found a corner of the living room where she could sit and examine the fringe of a carpet, tracing the patterns with her finger, completely absorbed in whatever she was discovering through this repetitive exploration.

My father called her name several times from across the room. "Enya," he said, then louder: "Enya, come to Baba."

Nothing. Not even a flicker of acknowledgment. She continued her examination of the carpet fringe as if she existed in a soundproof bubble.

My mother tried, then my wife, then me. We could have been calling to empty air for all the response we received. She wasn't defiant or deliberately ignoring us – she was in a different world altogether – pulling her hair strands at the top of her head, where she had her hair done in a neat small ponytail, and with both her eyes centering towards the top of her nose in between the eyebrows. She simply seemed unreachable through the ordinary channels of human communication.

"Something is wrong with her hearing," my father said finally, his voice heavy with concern. "This isn't normal behavior for a child her age."

The comparison was unavoidable and heartbreaking. Here was my sister's daughter, responding immediately every time someone called her name, running over when beckoned, engaging in the kind of back-and-forth interaction that seemed to come naturally to children her age. And here was Enya, completely absorbed in her own world, unreachable despite our increasingly desperate attempts to capture her attention.

"Look at how the other children respond," my mother observed quietly. "They look up when you call them. They come when you ask. They want to be part of what's happening."

"She used to do that," my wife said, and I heard the grief in her voice – the recognition that we were mourning something we had lost, not just struggling with something that had never existed.

"What happened to her?" my father asked, the question that had been haunting me for months but that I had been afraid to voice directly.

"I don't know," I admitted. "She was fine, and then after the vaccination, she just... changed."

"Maybe the shots were too much for her system," my mother suggested, articulating the hypothesis that had been forming in my mind. "Some children are more sensitive. Maybe her body couldn't handle it."

My mother insisted we get her hearing tested immediately. "We can't wait," she said. "If there's a problem, the earlier we catch it, the better. But looking at her now, compared to other children, I think it's more than hearing."

The next few weeks became a blur of medical appointments and tests. The BERA test required Enya to be sedated so they could measure her brain's response to sounds. Watching her small body lie still while machines measured neural activity felt like a violation of the natural, calm rhythm she had always moved to.

When the results came back showing normal hearing, I felt simultaneous relief and frustration. Her hearing was fine, so the problem wasn't what we had initially suspected. But if she could hear, why didn't she respond when we called her name?

The audiologist who delivered the results looked at us with an expression I was beginning to recognize in medical professionals – the careful neutrality of someone about to deliver news that would change everything.

"Her hearing is perfectly normal," he said carefully. "But given what you've described about her behavior and what I've observed during testing, I think you should have her evaluated for autism spectrum disorder."

Autism.

The word landed in the room like a stone dropped into still water, sending ripples through everything I thought I knew about my daughter's future. I had heard the term, but only in the vague way that parents hear about conditions they assume will never affect their own family.

"What is autism?" I asked, the question revealing just how unprepared I was for this possibility.

The explanation was clinical and careful: a developmental condition affecting communication and social interaction, characterized by repetitive behaviors and intense focus on specific interests. The symptoms he described – lack of eye contact, limited response to name, absorption in repetitive activities – sounded exactly like the daughter I was now living with.

"Could this be related to the vaccination?" I asked, giving voice to the question that had been haunting me since the transformation began.

"There's no scientific evidence of a causal relationship," he replied carefully. "But some children do show regression around the time of vaccinations. It's possible that she had subtle signs earlier that became more pronounced, or that some children are more susceptible to stressors on their developing systems."

My mother's tears that day were different from the others I had witnessed. Not the sharp grief of sudden loss, but the deep, ongoing sorrow of dreams that would never be realized.

"I keep thinking about the granddaughter I imagined," she said through her crying. "Teaching her to cook, listening to her tell me about her day."

"You can still do some of those things," I offered.

"Can I? She doesn't talk to me. She doesn't seem to see me."

This was the heart of her grief - not just the loss of typical grandparent experiences, but the fear that she would never have a relationship with this granddaughter at all.

"I love her," she said fiercely. "But I don't know how to love her in a way she can receive."

"Maybe we have to learn her language instead of teaching her ours."

"I'm sixty years old. I'm afraid I'm too old to learn new ways of loving."

***

In Mumbai, at a renowned developmental pediatrics center, another doctor confirmed what we had begun to suspect. "She's quite young for a formal diagnosis," he said, "and the criteria are complex. But yes, there are clear signs consistent with autism spectrum disorder."

"We're seeing some markers that suggest she's processing the world differently," he explained. "The lack of social engagement, the repetitive behaviors, the difficulty with typical communication – these are characteristic patterns."

"What does that mean for her future?" my wife asked, her voice steady but strained.

I found myself asking the question that revealed how little I understood: "Can this be... fixed?"

"Let's talk about support and understanding rather than fixing," the doctor replied gently. "Autism isn't something to cure – it's a different way of experiencing the world. Our job is to help her communicate and function while honoring how her mind works."

Suddenly my daughter had a new identity: autistic. It was her first real label beyond the basic categories of human existence – daughter, child, girl. And like all labels, it came with a complete package of assumptions, expectations, limitations, and prescribed responses.

But it also came with explanations for the transformation I had witnessed. The loss of eye contact, the retreat from social engagement, the intense focus on specific sensory experiences – these weren't random changes or temporary phases. They were expressions of a fundamentally different way of processing and responding to the world.

The grief I felt was complex and contradictory. I wasn't grieving for the child sitting beside me, who remained beautiful and mine and worthy of love. I was grieving for the future I had imagined, the easy path of typical development that was no longer available to us, the child I had known for fifteen months who seemed to have relocated to a place I couldn't follow.

"So now we have a word for it," my wife said as we drove home from the diagnosis appointment.

"Autism. Such a clinical word for something so... personal," I replied.

"Does it change who she is?"

"No. But it changes everything about how we understand who she is."

***

The well-meaning advice began immediately. "You should try this therapy." "I heard about a child who recovered completely." "Don't worry, I have seen that with early intervention, many children improve significantly."

Each suggestion carried the implicit message that our current reality was temporary, something to be overcome rather than understood. The assumption was that with enough effort, expertise, and intervention, we could bring back the child we had known for those first fifteen months.

But as we began the journey of therapies and treatments, I couldn't shake the feeling that we were missing something essential. The engaging baby hadn't disappeared—she had transformed into someone who engaged with the world according to entirely different principles. Instead of trying to reverse the transformation, maybe we needed to learn the language of who she had become.

The diagnosis was the beginning, not the end, of our real education. It opened the door to understanding that intelligence and connection come in forms I had never imagined, that love doesn't require eye contact to be real, and that some of the most profound teachers speak without words.

I didn't know yet that the daughter I thought I had lost would eventually teach me more about presence, authenticity, and consciousness itself than the engaging baby ever could have. I didn't understand that what looked like regression might actually be a different kind of progression—one that would challenge every assumption I held about communication, intelligence, and what makes a meaningful human life.

But the door had opened, and there was no going back to the simple certainties of typical development. Our journey into the mystery of a different kind of mind – and the discovery of forms of wisdom our culture had forgotten how to recognize – was just beginning.

Labels create the illusion of understanding while often obscuring living reality. "Autism" became a cognitive container that allowed us to feel we knew something about her condition while actually organizing our confusion into manageable concepts.

This experience taught me to distinguish between descriptive utility and explanatory power. Labels can be useful for accessing services, finding community, and organizing observations – but they become dangerous when we mistake them for complete understanding. The map is never the territory.

2. The Day the Family Cried

When other children laughed,
my heart broke
not for her pain
but for my own blindness.

It wasn't really a single day when the family cried. It was more like a season of tears that had been building since that sudden transformation when she was fifteen months old, a gradual reckoning with what her differences would mean as she grew older and the world's expectations grew stronger.

But if I had to choose one moment when the full weight of our new reality became undeniably visible, it would be that afternoon at the neighborhood park when Enya was three years old.

We had been living with her post-transformation self for well over a year by then. The engaging baby who had connected so naturally with us had been replaced by a child who found her connection through different channels – textures, patterns, repetitive movements that brought her obvious satisfaction but looked foreign to casual observers.

I had taken her to the playground that day hoping that being around other children might spark some form of social engagement, even though we knew by now that her way of connecting with the world operated according to different principles than theirs.

Enya was drawn, as always, to the periphery. While the other children ran toward the swings and slides, she found a patch of grass where she could sit and examine the texture of bark on a nearby tree. She had discovered a small depression in the trunk where the wood formed interesting patterns, and she was tracing these with her finger, completely absorbed in whatever information she was gathering from the tactile exploration.

A group of children, probably four or five years old, noticed her sitting alone. At first, they seemed curious rather than cruel. One little boy approached and said something to her. When she didn't respond – hadn't responded to children her age since the transformation – he tried again, louder. Then he began making exaggerated faces, trying to capture her attention.

When that didn't work, the children began to laugh.

It started as innocent amusement – the kind of laughter children make when they encounter something they don't understand. But as more children gathered, the laughter took on a different quality. They began imitating her posture, the way she held her head tilted while examining the bark. One child stuck his tongue out slightly, mimicking the expression she sometimes made when concentrating deeply.

They weren't being deliberately malicious. They were just children responding to difference the way children do – with curiosity that can quickly become mockery when they can't make sense of what they're seeing.

But watching it happen, sitting on a bench twenty feet away, I felt something crack open in my chest. A kind of agony I had never experienced before – not just the helpless heartbreak of a parent witnessing their child being mocked, but something deeper. The recognition that this was what the world would see when it looked at the daughter I had learned to love in her transformed state.

Enya, for her part, seemed completely unaware of the children around her. She continued her examination of the bark patterns with the same focused attention she might have given to any other interesting texture. Their laughter, their imitations, their attempts to engage her – none of it penetrated the bubble of her own absorption.

Which somehow made it more painful. Not because I wanted her to be hurt by their mockery, but because the gap between her reality and theirs seemed so vast. She was operating according to completely different principles – following her own curiosity, finding beauty in details others overlooked, content in her own sensory experience. They were following the social scripts of childhood – seeking connection through shared play, responding to difference with teasing when they couldn't understand it.

I walked over and gently guided Enya to a different part of the playground, away from the small crowd that had gathered. But the moment had crystallized something we had been living with but not fully acknowledging: this was how the world would see her, and this was how we would need to protect her from a world that didn't understand her way of being.

That evening, when I called my parents to share what had happened. It was meant to be a simple update, but it turned into something else entirely – a collective confrontation with what Enya's transformed state would mean for all of us as she grew older.

My mother cried first. Not the gentle tears of sympathy, but the deep, body-shaking sobs of someone who had been carrying grief for over a year without fully processing it.

"I keep thinking about the baby she was," she said through her tears. "The way she used to look at us, respond to us. Where did that little girl go?"

This was the heart of our family's ongoing grief. We weren't just struggling with having a different child – we were mourning the loss of the engaging, responsive baby we had known and loved for fifteen months. The child who sat before us was beautiful and ours, but she wasn't the same person who had gazed into our eyes with such focused attention during her first year.

"Why did this happen to her?" my mother continued. "She was perfect, and then..."

"And then something changed her," my father finished, giving voice to the question that had haunted our family since the transformation. "Something took away the child we knew."

I found myself trying to comfort them while simultaneously struggling with my own unresolved grief about the daughter we had lost and the challenge of learning to love the daughter we now had.

My father had responded to the transformation by consulting astrologers and healers, searching for cosmic explanations or spiritual remedies that might reverse what had happened. "One astrologer says there are planetary influences that can be corrected," he would tell me during our phone conversations. "Another suggests specific ceremonies that might help bring her back."

"Bring her back to what, Papa?" I asked during one of these calls. "She's not the same child she was at fifteen months. We have to learn to love who she is now."

"But she was so bright before," he replied. "So engaged. That has to still be in there somewhere."

My wife's grief had evolved into fierce protectiveness mixed with practical worry. "What happens when she gets older and the other children are even crueler?" she would ask. "What happens when she's a teenager and the social expectations become impossible for her to meet?"

These questions felt both urgently important and impossibly distant. Enya was three years old. But the playground incident had shown us a preview of every future social situation where her differences would be visible and misunderstood.

"She doesn't suffer the way we do," I found myself saying during one family conversation. "She seems content in her own world. We're the ones who are struggling."

"But what about friends, relationships, a normal life?" my sister asked.

"Maybe normal isn't what we should be hoping for anymore," I replied, beginning to articulate something I was still learning to understand.

Each family member seemed to be processing this ongoing reality through their own lens of loss and hope. My wife researched intensive therapies and intervention programs, maintaining determined optimism that the right combination of treatments might help Enya reconnect with the world in more conventional ways.

My brother approached it practically, asking detailed questions about therapies and long-term planning, wanting to understand how he could help support a niece whose needs were unlike anything our family had experienced before.

"I wish I understood what happened," he said during one visit. "She was such a responsive baby, and then..."

"And then she became someone else," I finished. "Someone we're still learning to know."

But beneath everyone's different coping strategies was the same fundamental grief: we had lost the child we thought we were going to raise and found ourselves learning to love a completely different person who happened to live in the same body.

The playground incident became a kind of template for how we learned to navigate public spaces with her. We developed strategies: choosing less crowded times, selecting activities where her unique interests might be less conspicuous, preparing responses for curious or insensitive comments from other parents.

We were learning to live with a different kind of vigilance – not just protecting her from harm, but protecting her dignity from a world that didn't understand that her way of being was valid, even if it looked different from what people expected.

The irony, which I couldn't see then, was that Enya herself seemed largely unaffected by these encounters with the world's lack of understanding. The children's laughter at the playground hadn't disturbed her peace any more than their acceptance would have enhanced it. She was operating from a different center, one that didn't depend on external validation for its stability.

But we couldn't access that center. We were too caught up in our own projections about what her differences would mean for her happiness, her future, her place in a world that seemed determined to measure everyone against the same narrow standards.

The family tears were really tears for multiple losses: the engaging baby we had known and loved, the conventional future we had imagined for her, the easy path of typical development that was no longer available to any of us. We were grieving what she had been while struggling to learn how to love what she had become.

We cried because we didn't yet understand that some of life's most profound gifts come disguised as losses, and that the journey from seeing her transformation as a tragedy to recognizing it as a different kind of gift would require us to question everything we thought we knew about intelligence, connection, and what makes a life meaningful.

It would take years for me to stop trying to find the engaging baby hidden inside the transformed child and start appreciating the unique intelligence and awareness that had emerged from her different way of processing the world. To recognize that we hadn't lost a daughter – we had been given the opportunity to love a completely different kind of consciousness, one that would teach us things the engaging baby never could have.

But those realizations were still far in the future. For now, there were only the tears for what we had lost, the questions about why it had happened, and the slow, difficult process of learning to protect and celebrate a child whose way of being challenged every assumption we held about development, connection, and love.

The day the family cried wasn't really about the playground incident. It was about finally allowing ourselves to feel the full weight of a transformation that had changed not just Enya, but all of us. We had to grieve the loss of who she had been before we could fully embrace who she had become.

She continued to trace patterns in tree bark, to examine textures with focused attention, to find beauty and meaning in sensory experiences that others overlooked. She was already living in a different relationship with reality—one that would eventually become our teacher if we could learn to receive rather than resist the wisdom she was offering through her transformed way of being.

3. Therapies and Thresholds

I gathered experts like weapons
to fight a war
that existed only
in my mind.

The therapy phase of our lives began with the kind of determined optimism that only parents in crisis can muster. If Enya had autism, then we would find the best interventions. If she wasn't developing typically, then we would provide her with every possible tool and support until she did.

My entire life reorganized itself around her needs. Work became secondary to research about autism therapies. Weekends were consumed by appointments and evaluations. Every conversation with other parents became an opportunity to gather intelligence about what was working, what was showing promise, what might be the key that unlocked her potential.

Our movement from Mumbai to New Delhi was partially fueled by this determination. At Action for Autism in Delhi, we met our first team of specialists. The speech therapist was a kind woman who spoke with the gentle confidence of someone who had seen progress in the most challenging cases.

"We'll work on increasing verbal communication," she explained during our initial consultation, showing us cards with simple images. "Apple. Ball. Cat. The goal is to build from single sounds to words to simple sentences."

"How long does this usually take?" I asked, already calculating timelines and measuring progress.

"There's no timeline. Every child progresses differently," she replied with the patience of someone who had answered this question countless times.

"Translation: we have no idea," I thought to myself, though I nodded politely.

Enya sat at the small table, her attention drifting to the way the fluorescent light created patterns on the laminated cards. When the therapist held up the apple picture and said "A-a-apple," Enya's eyes followed the movement of her mouth with what seemed like genuine interest. For a moment, I felt a surge of hope. Maybe this would be easier than we thought.

But weeks passed with no sounds emerging. The therapist remained encouraging, adjusting her approach, trying different techniques. "Some children take longer to find their voice," she assured us. "The important thing is consistency."

Consistency became our religion. Three times a week for speech therapy. Twice a week for occupational therapy, where another gentle specialist worked on sensory integration, fine motor skills, and something called "purposeful play."

During one occupational therapy session, I found myself observing more carefully than usual. The therapist noted Enya's remarkable fine motor control.

"She has excellent fine motor skills," the OT observed, watching Enya manipulate small objects with precision.

"But she won't hold a crayon properly," my wife pointed out, a note of frustration in her voice.

"She holds it the way that works for her," the therapist replied. "Maybe we're the ones who need to adapt."

This comment stayed with me during our drive home.

***

"Three therapies a week," my wife said as we navigated Delhi traffic.

"Plus preschool," I added.

"When does she get to just be a kid?" she asked, voicing something I had been thinking but hadn't articulated.

"Maybe therapy is how she gets to be herself," I suggested, though I was beginning to wonder if the opposite might be true.

During these sessions, I began to notice things that the formal assessments weren't capturing. The way Enya's whole body would relax when she encountered certain textures. How she would smile – just barely, but definitely smile – when she figured out how to manipulate a particularly interesting toy. The quiet satisfaction on her face when she completed a task in her own way, even if it wasn't the way the therapist had intended.

But these observations felt secondary to the main goal, which was progress. Measurable, documentable, clearly defined progress toward typical development.

***

When the conventional therapies didn't yield the dramatic results we hoped for, we expanded our search. My father's network of astrologers and healers suddenly became relevant in ways I had never imagined. If modern medicine had limitations, perhaps ancient wisdom could fill the gaps.

The Ayurvedic doctor from Rajasthan examined Enya with a completely different framework, feeling her pulse, observing her constitution, prescribing herbal medicines designed to "balance her doshas." The treatment involved giving her bitter-tasting powders three times a day, following specific dietary restrictions, and applying oils to particular pressure points.

Enya tolerated these interventions with remarkable patience, though she had her own ways of expressing preferences. She would spit out medicines she found particularly objectionable, but would accept others without resistance. I began to wonder if she had some intuitive sense of what her body needed, operating from a wisdom that bypassed rational analysis.

Then there was the healer who claimed that pressing specific points on her fingertips could stimulate brain development. We drove across the city so this man could hold Enya's small fingers and apply pressure to points that corresponded, he said, to different areas of cognitive function.

The homeopathic doctor prescribed tiny white pills that dissolved under her tongue, designed to help correct her developmental delays. The treatment required precise timing – certain pills at specific hours, nothing to eat or drink for fifteen minutes before and after each dose.

Through all of these interventions, Enya maintained an essential quality that I was too focused on outcomes to fully appreciate at the time. She remained present to her own experience in a way that was remarkably uncompromised by our efforts to change her.

When she was supposed to be practicing speech sounds, she might instead become fascinated by the texture of the therapy table, running her fingers along its surface with obvious pleasure. When she was supposed to be building with blocks according to the occupational therapist's instructions, she might arrange them in patterns that followed some aesthetic logic invisible to the rest of us but clearly meaningful to her.

There were moments when I caught glimpses of something that challenged the entire premise of our intervention efforts. Like the time she figured out how to operate my laptop, not through the standard point-and-click method we were trying to teach her, but by discovering other ways to produce interesting visual effects on the screen. She spent an hour creating patterns and colors, completely absorbed in what was clearly, to her, a form of play.

But these moments felt like distractions from the real work of helping her develop normal communication and social skills. I would gently redirect her attention back to the approved activities, the ones that would lead to measurable progress.

***

The grand puja was my father's idea. If individual healing approaches weren't sufficient, perhaps a more comprehensive spiritual intervention was needed. He organized a ceremony with dozens of pandits, elaborate rituals, hours of Sanskrit chanting designed to invoke divine assistance for Enya's development.

Enya sat through the entire ceremony with remarkable composure, occasionally reaching out to touch the brass vessels or examine the flower petals being scattered around the fire. She seemed more interested in the sensory aspects of the ritual – the sounds, textures, visual patterns – than in whatever spiritual transformation it was supposed to facilitate.

I found myself caught between genuine hope that divine intervention might help and growing skepticism about our assumption that she needed to be fundamentally different from who she was.

The mantras came next. Specific Sanskrit phrases that we were supposed to recite a certain number of times each day. The gemstones – particular stones worn in precise configurations to enhance cognitive development. The blessed water from conch shells, which we were told would purify her system and open pathways for normal development.

She even had a coach to teach her how to pedal her tricycle.

This last intervention felt particularly absurd in retrospect. Here was a child who could spend hours creating complex visual patterns with household objects, who had developed her own sophisticated systems for categorizing and organizing the world around her, and we were worried that she couldn't pedal a tricycle according to standard developmental timelines.

But at the time, every milestone felt crucial. Every delay seemed like evidence that we weren't doing enough, trying hard enough, finding the right combination of interventions that would unlock her potential.

One evening, during bath time, I found myself speaking directly to her about all the people trying to help.

"So many people want to help you speak their language. What if we learned yours instead?" I said as she played happily in the water.

She splashed contentedly, and I took that as confirmation.

"I'll take that as a yes."

The assumption underlying all these efforts was that focused attention and persistent effort could overcome any obstacle. This was the worldview I had brought from my professional life – where all complex problems require comprehensive solutions, and with enough resources and determination, any challenge can be met.

***

During therapy sessions, I began to notice that her attention would sometimes shift in ways that revealed profound awareness. She would look directly at the therapist's face when she sensed frustration, offering what seemed like comfort through eye contact. She would become particularly gentle and still when she could sense that someone in the room was upset.

These moments of connection were unlike anything the formal assessments were measuring, but they suggested a form of emotional intelligence that was far more sophisticated than her inability to speak might indicate.

Yet these observations felt secondary to the main project of helping her develop the skills that would allow her to function in the world as it existed, rather than questioning whether the world as it existed had any room for the kind of intelligence she was demonstrating.

The message from every direction – medical, educational, social – was clear: conform or struggle. Develop typical skills or face lifelong limitation. Learn to communicate in conventional ways or remain isolated from meaningful human connection.

But something in me was beginning to question this framework, though I couldn't yet articulate what felt wrong about it. The more I watched Enya navigate these interventions with such grace and presence, the more I wondered whether the problem was her inability to adapt to our expectations or our inability to recognize the validity of her way of being.

But the seeds of a different understanding were already being planted. In the spaces between therapy sessions, in the moments when she was free to follow her own interests, in the quiet demonstrations of awareness and intelligence that didn't fit any of our categories, she was beginning to show me that the real question wasn't how to help her fit into our world.

The real question was whether our world had any room for the kind of wisdom she was offering.

***

The Rhythm of Repetition

By her fifth year, Enya had developed what I initially saw as an elaborate collection of symptoms that needed to be managed. What I couldn't yet understand was that she was actually creating a sophisticated system of rituals that brought order to a world that often felt chaotic and overwhelming.

Her day began with a precise sequence that never varied. Upon waking, she would first examine the texture of her bedsheet, running her fingers along the fabric in long, methodical strokes. Then she would arrange her things in a specific configuration – largest to smallest, sorted by color, positioned at exact angles that made sense only to her.

I was caught between trying to respect these routines and feeling compelled to interrupt them. The therapists had warned us about "perseverative behaviors" and the importance of introducing flexibility.

"She gets upset when we change the daily schedule," her preschool teacher mentioned during a conference.

"So don't change it," I replied, thinking this was obvious.

"But children need to learn flexibility," the teacher insisted.

"Maybe they need to learn that some minds thrive on consistency," I countered, beginning to question whether flexibility was always a virtue.

So, I would gently redirect her attention when the bedsheet examination went on too long. I would suggest alternative arrangements for the stuffed animals. I would try to introduce small variations to her morning routine, believing I was helping her develop resilience and adaptability.

But every interruption seemed to cost her something essential. When I moved one of her carefully positioned dolls, she would patiently return it to its proper place, then begin the entire process again from the beginning. When I hurried her through the fabric examination, she would return to it later, as if she needed to complete some internal requirement that my intervention had disrupted.

Her relationship with repetition extended far beyond morning routines. She had discovered that our living room had a perfect circuit for walking – from the couch to the dining table to the window and back. She would walk this path dozens of times each day, sometimes pausing to examine interesting shadows or light patterns, sometimes maintaining a steady rhythm that seemed almost meditative.

I became her walking partner by default. Morning, afternoon, evening – whenever she headed toward the door with that particular expression of focused intention, I knew she was ready for one of our circuits.

During one of our evening walks, I met a man who came up to me and said he had a kid who was recently diagnosed autistic.

"This is so overwhelming. How do you do it?"

"One day at a time. Some days, one hour at a time.", I said.

"Does it get easier?"

I smiled: "It gets different. You get stronger. You learn to see gifts where you once saw deficits."

***

Initially, I saw these walks as opportunities for interaction, chances to work on communication skills or social connection. "Look, Enya," I would say, pointing to a bird or a flower or another child. "Do you see that?"

But I gradually realized that she had her own agenda for these walks, her own way of gathering information about the world that didn't depend on my commentary or direction. She would stop at specific trees, not because I had pointed them out, but because something about their bark pattern or the way light filtered through their leaves had captured her attention.

Her attraction to certain objects and places seemed random at first, but over time I began to see patterns. She was drawn to textures with regular repetition—brick walls, chain-link fences, corrugated surfaces. She would spend long minutes running her fingers along these patterns, and something about her expression suggested she was receiving information that the rest of us couldn't access.

This led to what the family euphemistically called her "wandering phase." The moment she was left unattended, she would drift toward whatever had captured her interest – the next shop with an interesting storefront, the next street with appealing visual patterns. We learned to hold her hand carefully, not because she was trying to escape, but because her attention operated according to different principles than ours.

What looked like impulsivity to us was actually a sophisticated form of environmental exploration. She wasn't wandering aimlessly; she was following a kind of magnetic attraction to specific visual, tactile, or auditory experiences that served some purpose in her internal organization.

But perhaps the most profound of her rituals was what became our evening tradition: she would climb onto my shoulders and reach up to touch the ceiling. This simple game became the most reliable source of pure joy in both our lives.

Standing on my shoulders, arms stretched high, fingertips brushing the textured ceiling, she would laugh with a kind of abandon that seemed to come from somewhere deep inside her. Not the social laughter of shared jokes or funny faces, but the spontaneous expression of a being encountering exactly the sensory experience it craved.

For me, these moments became islands of uncomplicated connection in an ocean of therapeutic interventions and developmental concerns. When she was on my shoulders, reaching for the ceiling, we weren't working on goals or practicing skills. We were simply sharing an experience that brought her obvious pleasure and gave me the rare gift of seeing her completely at ease in her own body.

During our bedtime routine one evening, I found myself reflecting on these patterns.

"Same three books, same order, same songs," I said to my wife as we tucked Enya in.

"For eight months now," my wife replied.

"You think we should mix it up?"

My wife watched Enya's peaceful expression as she arranged her stuffed animals in their nighttime arrangement. "Why fix what isn't broken?"

But even this beloved ritual came under scrutiny from well-meaning professionals. "Be careful not to reinforce repetitive behaviors," one therapist warned. "It's important to help her develop a broader range of interests and activities."

I found myself caught in an impossible contradiction. Should I continue the ceiling-touching game because it was one of the few activities where she seemed genuinely joyful? Or should I gradually phase it out to encourage more varied forms of play?

The contradiction felt impossible to resolve through rational analysis. Every approach seemed to sacrifice something important. If I supported her natural rhythms and preferences, I worried I was limiting her potential for growth. If I pushed for more conventional forms of engagement, I felt like I was asking her to abandon the very things that brought structure and meaning to her experience.

Watching Enya intensely watch a tree in the wind from our balcony one afternoon, I was taken aback. "I called it obsession," I thought to myself. "But watching her now... this isn't compulsion. This is mastery. This is her meditation."

What I would gradually realize was that Enya's repetitive behaviors weren't symptoms to be managed or deficits to be corrected. They were expressions of a profound intelligence that operated through rhythm, pattern, and sensory integration rather than through language and social interaction. The walking circuits were moving meditations that helped her process and integrate the countless sensory inputs she encountered throughout the day.

She was already living what I would spend years trying to learn: how to find stillness within movement, how to create order without rigidity, how to be fully present to immediate sensory experience without being overwhelmed by it.

But in year five, I was still trapped in trying to interrupt these patterns rather than learning from them. I couldn't yet see that her repetitions were actually teaching me about the intelligence of rhythm, the wisdom of patterns, the possibility of finding peace through purposeful movement.

There were moments when I caught glimpses of something that challenged my entire framework for understanding her behavior. Like the time she discovered that running water from the bathroom faucet created different sounds depending on the angle and pressure, and spent an hour conducting what could only be described as a water symphony, her face lit up with the concentrated pleasure of someone making music.

These moments revealed an aesthetic intelligence that operated outside all our therapeutic goals and educational objectives. She was creating beauty, finding patterns, making meaning through direct sensory engagement with the world. But I didn't yet have categories for recognizing this as intelligence, much less as a form of wisdom that I might learn from.

Year five was when I began to feel the real education in our relationship might be flowing in the opposite direction from what I had thought. But thoughts still ruled and these feelings may have moved me at an unconscious level.

Her life and activities were touching me at some level and teaching me about the intelligence of attention, of watching without thoughts, the possibility that what we call limitation might sometimes be a form of mastery that we simply don't know how to recognize. But this unconscious realization still needed to break through to the conscious levels of clarity and realization.

***

When Play Teaches More Than Words

By her sixth year, Enya had developed what I can only describe as a PhD-level expertise in the art of finding wonder in the overlooked details of ordinary life. While other children her age were learning to play with toys according to their intended purposes, she was discovering that the most fascinating playground existed in the spaces between conventional categories.

Her approach to play challenged every assumption I held about childhood development and learning. Where educational toys were designed to teach specific skills through predetermined activities, she found infinite entertainment in exploring the properties of light, shadow, texture, water, and sound that existed everywhere around us.

For example, her relationship with our collection of metal drinking glasses. While we saw them as functional objects for holding beverages, she had discovered that each glass produced a different musical tone when tapped, that the sound changed depending on how much water it contained, and that the reflective surfaces created fascinating visual patterns when light hit them from different angles.

The one time a glass slipped from the kitchen counter and crashed to the floor, she went into what appeared to be sensory overload – covering her ears, rocking back and forth, tears streaming down her face. At the time, I interpreted this as evidence of her difficulty processing unexpected sounds. But I was beginning to suspect there was more to it than simple auditory sensitivity.

She had developed such a refined appreciation for the subtle musical qualities of those glasses that the harsh, chaotic sound was like hearing a beautiful instrument being destroyed. It wasn't just loud – it seemed wrong, a violation of the harmonic principles she had been studying through her gentle explorations, though I will never know this for sure.

This incident taught me something crucial about the difference between her play and the structured activities we were encouraging in therapy. When she was freely exploring the glasses, experimenting with their sounds and visual properties, she was completely absorbed, peaceful, obviously learning something important. When we tried to redirect her attention to "appropriate" uses of those same objects, she became restless and disconnected.

The joy wasn't in the objects themselves – it was in her approach to discovering their hidden properties.

"Want to play catch?" I asked her one afternoon, holding up a colorful ball that was supposed to encourage typical play behaviors.

She picked up the ball, examined it carefully, then placed it precisely on a shelf – not dismissively, but with the same careful attention she brought to all her arrangements.

"That's... not how you play catch," I said, feeling the futility of the correction even as I spoke.

She smiled, raised her hands and made a sound with a short laughter – her version of sharing joy in the moment, regardless of whether her joy matched my expectations.

"But you're happy. So maybe it is how you play catch," I realized, beginning to question my definitions of correct play.

Our first trip to a shopping mall provided another window into her unique way of processing the world. While I expected her to be excited by the toys and colors and activity, she instead became completely overwhelmed by what I initially saw as the chaos of too much stimulation.

She stood in the main corridor, staring upward at the elaborate lighting fixtures, tears beginning to form in her eyes. But as I watched more carefully, I realized she wasn't crying from distress – she was crying from a kind of aesthetic overload. The endless patterns of lights, the way they reflected and refracted off the polished surfaces, the complex interplay of artificial and natural illumination – it was too much beauty to process all at once.

While other children were drawn to the toy stores and candy shops, she was receiving a graduate-level education in architecture, engineering, and visual design simply by standing still and letting her senses absorb the sophisticated patterns that adults had stopped noticing.

This was when I began to understand that her way of playing with the world was actually a form of research. She wasn't randomly attracted to objects and experiences – she was conducting systematic investigations into the fundamental properties of matter, energy, space, and time.

At the playground, I watched this research methodology in action.

"Want to go down the slide, Enya?" I asked, pointing to the equipment designed for typical childhood recreation.

She sat at the bottom of the slide instead, running sand through her fingers with the intense focus of someone studying particle physics.

"Is she okay?" another parent asked, concern evident in their voice.

"She's perfect. She's studying gravity," I replied, beginning to see her activities through a different lens.

Her favorite "game," if it could be called that, was our daily exploration walks. Every morning, afternoon, and evening, she would head toward the door with that particular expression of focused intention, and I learned to recognize this as an invitation to join her in discovering something new about our immediate environment.

These weren't walks in the conventional sense – purposeful movement from one location to another. They were more like mobile meditation sessions, opportunities for her to gather sensory information that she would later process and integrate through her various rituals and repetitive behaviors.

She would stop abruptly at a chain-link fence, spending several minutes running her fingers along the regular diamond patterns. Or she would be drawn to a particular tree, not because I had pointed it out, but because something about the texture of its bark or the pattern of its branches had captured her attention.

I gradually learned to follow her lead rather than trying to direct these explorations. When I let her set the pace and choose the destinations, the walks became profound lessons in attention and presence. She was teaching me how to notice things I had walked past hundreds of times without seeing.

The therapeutic playgroups we attended provided stark contrast to her natural way of learning. In these structured environments, children were expected to play with toys in predetermined ways, to engage in social interactions according to specific scripts, to demonstrate progress through measurable improvements in conventional play skills.

Enya would sit at the edge of these activities, not because she was withdrawn or antisocial, but because she was conducting a different kind of research. While the other children were learning to use blocks to build towers, she was studying the way light created geometric shadows when blocks were arranged in certain configurations.

The play therapist would gently encourage her to join the group activities, to use toys "appropriately," to engage in the kind of parallel play that was considered developmentally appropriate for her age. But I began to notice that her independent explorations were far more sophisticated than anything happening in the organized activities.

When left to her own devices, she would create complex arrangements of ordinary objects—bottle caps sorted by color and size, pebbles arranged in mathematical patterns, leaves organized according to shape and texture. These creations revealed an aesthetic intelligence that operated according to principles I couldn't fully understand but was beginning to recognize as valid.

At the toy store, this difference became particularly apparent.

"She's ignored every toy and spent twenty minutes with the box," my wife observed with amusement.

"Should we buy the box?" I asked, only half-joking.

"Why not? She's happier with it than most kids are with the toy."

Her relationship with water became another avenue for understanding her unique approach to learning. While other children splashed and played in conventional ways, she discovered that water was actually a sophisticated medium for exploring physics, acoustics, and visual phenomena.

She could spend an hour at the bathroom sink, adjusting the faucet pressure to create different sounds, holding her hand at various angles to change the flow patterns, watching with fascination as light refracted through the moving water. To an observer, it might have looked like she was just playing with water. But she was actually conducting experiments in fluid dynamics that would have impressed any engineer.

What I was learning was that her joy didn't depend on external validation or social approval. She could find profound satisfaction in activities that others might find boring or meaningless. Her happiness came from some internal source that was activated by certain types of sensory experience and discovery.

This was both inspiring and challenging for me as a parent. On one hand, I was amazed by her capacity for self-directed learning and independent contentment. On the other hand, I worried about how this would translate into success in a world that values collaborative play, social interaction, and conformity to established educational approaches.

During therapy sessions focused on "play skills," I would watch professionals try to teach her how to engage with toys in ways that would prepare her for typical childhood social interactions.

They meant well, and some of their strategies were helpful. But I was beginning to see that her natural play style was actually more sophisticated than what they were trying to teach her.

She didn't need to learn how to play – she needed to be recognized for the profound forms of learning she was already engaged in through her unique approach to exploration and discovery.

At the dinner table one evening, I tried to share what I was observing.

"Let's play 'What did you do today?'" I suggested, hoping to encourage some form of conventional social interaction.

Enya picked up her spoon, examined it carefully, then tapped it rhythmically against her bowl – creating a complex percussion pattern that seemed to delight her.

"I think she just told us," my wife said with a smile.

"She discovered music in a spoon. That's poetry," I replied, finally beginning to appreciate the sophistication of her communications.

Her play was teaching me that intelligence comes in many forms, that learning doesn't always look like what we expect, and that some of the most important education happens when children are free to follow their own curiosity rather than predetermined curricula.

But perhaps most importantly, she was demonstrating that joy and wisdom often emerge from the same source – a willingness to be fully present to immediate experience without needing it to be anything other than what it is.

During a quiet moment at bedtime, I found myself speaking directly to her about what I was learning.

"You don't play like other kids," I said as she carefully arranged her blocks in their precise nighttime configuration.

She looked up from her work, offering me that direct gaze that always seemed to convey understanding.

"You play like a scientist. Like an artist. Like someone who sees magic where others see ordinary."

By the end of her sixth year, I was beginning to suspect that the real education in our relationship was flowing from her to me. She was teaching me about presence, about the intelligence of direct sensory engagement, about finding wonder in the overlooked details of ordinary life.

But I was still years away from fully understanding that her way of playing with the world might be more sophisticated than our efforts to teach her conventional play skills. That her joy in simple sensory experiences might be pointing toward a different relationship with learning altogether – one based on intrinsic curiosity rather than external goals, on direct discovery rather than secondhand instruction.

She was already living this truth, finding contentment and fascination regardless of whether her activities produced results that others could recognize or measure.

***

PART II: THE AWAKENING

Eighteen Years with Enya

Clueless Years

She smiled at me

For a change, I could see…

She had smiled as a baby

Had captured it in pics

She kept on smiling easy

While I focused on the clicks…

Years had passed that I'd seen

Her smile that had been

Not that she ever stopped

But then, on my career was I focused…

Her future, her life, her shape & size

I was concerned of course!

I looked at her pics and,

She sat by my side…

Now seeing me see, her eyes widened

Amar B. Singh

A sunflower looking up at the sun risen

All the books, all the talks…
Useless pursuits, the pics in the stock

Quick realization… I smiled at her
Deeply sorry, my eyes may have told her

She smiled back, reassuringly
I realized I had not been me…

4. A Week with Enya - The Electric Shock

Seven days of paying attention
undid seven years
of sleeping
with my eyes open.

December 2015. Christmas vacation week. My wife was still working, caught up in year-end projects that couldn't wait for holidays. I found myself in the unusual position of being alone with Enya for an entire week—no therapies scheduled, no interventions planned, no agenda beyond simply being present with my eight-year-old daughter.

For the first time in eight years, I would discover what it meant to actually be with her rather than mentally somewhere else while physically in the same room.

The irony wasn't lost on me that I needed a vacation from my normal routine to spend uninterrupted time with my own child. But as the week began, I started to understand just how absent I had been, even during our daily interactions. My mind had always been partially occupied with work concerns, therapy schedules, developmental goals, or simply the mental noise of a life lived in constant planning mode.

This week would be different. With no immediate pressures or obligations, I committed to following her lead, seeing what emerged when I wasn't trying to direct or improve or teach anything. I had no idea I was about to receive the most important education of my life.

The first few days unfolded with a different quality of attention than I had ever brought to our time together. Instead of half-listening while mentally composing emails, I found myself actually hearing the subtle sounds she made—not words, but a kind of musical vocalization that seemed to match her internal rhythms.

Instead of glancing at her activities while thinking about other things, I began to really observe what she was doing. And what I saw challenged every assumption I had about her limitations and my role as her father.

She had been smiling all along. Not just the reflexive social smiles that caregivers look for, but genuine expressions of contentment, curiosity, even humor that I had been too distracted to notice. The realization hit me like a physical blow: I had been documenting her life through photographs while missing the actual experience of being with her.

She smiled at me
For a change, I could see...
She had smiled as a baby
Had captured it in pics
She kept on smiling easy
While I focused on the clicks...

Wednesday afternoon brought the moment that would crystallize everything. I was sitting on the couch, scrolling through photos on my phone—hundreds of images of Enya from the past few months, carefully catalogued memories of moments I thought I had been present for.

She was sitting right beside me.

I became aware that she was watching me look at pictures of herself. The irony was so stark it felt like touching a live wire. Here I was, studying documentation of my daughter's life while the living reality of her presence was inches away from me.

"Eight years of photos. Eight years of trying to capture her looking 'normal,'" I found myself thinking, still scrolling through the images.

When I looked up from the phone, our eyes met with an intensity that felt completely new. It was as if she was seeing me actually see her for the first time in years. Her eyes widened with what I can only describe as recognition—not just of my face, but of my presence, my actual attention finally landing fully on who she was in that moment.

She was sitting there, patient as always, waiting for me to notice that she was more interesting than any picture of her could ever be.

"You were never supposed to be normal, were you?" I said aloud, more to myself than to her.

She leaned against my shoulder – a simple gesture that felt like forgiveness and invitation combined.

"You were supposed to be exactly this."

In that instant, something fundamental shifted. All the books I had read about autism, all the theories about her limitations, all the interventions designed to help her connect—none of them had prepared me for the depth of awareness I encountered in her presence. She wasn't the one who had been absent or disconnected. I was.

Years had passed that I'd seen
Her smile that had been
Not that she ever stopped
But then, on my career was I focused...

Her future, her life, her shape & size
I was concerned of course!
I looked at her pics and,
She sat by my side...

The smile that followed was unlike any exchange we had ever had. There was forgiveness in it, patience, even a kind of gentle humor, as if she had been waiting for me to wake up and was relieved that it had finally happened. She seemed to understand that I had been sleepwalking through our relationship, and her smile conveyed both acceptance of this fact and joy that it was changing.

Over the remaining days of that week, I began to understand the deepest truth of our relationship. For eight years, I had been trying to change her—to make her more verbal, more social, more conventionally responsive. But the real transformation was happening in reverse. She was changing me, teaching me about presence, about the difference between documentation and experience, about forms of intelligence that operate outside the frameworks I thought I understood.

I had been the stone, trying to redirect the flow of her natural way of being. But she had been the patient water, gradually wearing away my rigid assumptions about communication, learning, and what makes a meaningful connection. The harder I had tried to change her direction, the more deeply she had been transforming my understanding of intelligence itself.

Now seeing me see, her eyes widened
A sunflower looking up at the sun risen
All the books, all the talks...
Useless pursuits, the pics in the stock
Quick realization... I smiled at her
Deeply sorry, my eyes may have told her
She smiled back, reassuringly
I realized I had not been me...

That week taught me that I had been approaching our relationship from a position of ego rather than openness. I had positioned myself as the teacher and her as the student, when the reality was exactly the opposite. She had been demonstrating a way of being present that I couldn't access through all my mental activity and planning.

The insights came rapidly once I stopped trying to manage or improve the situation and simply paid attention to what was actually happening. I realized that my attempts to help her "fit into society" were based on the assumption that society's way of organizing reality was superior to hers. But what if the opposite was true?

She moved through the world with a kind of presence that I had lost somewhere in my adult obsession with goals and achievements. While I was constantly planning, analyzing, worrying about future outcomes, she was fully inhabiting each moment, finding beauty and meaning in immediate sensory experience.

The Framework That Changed Everything

During this week, I began to understand what I would later recognize as different levels of consciousness operating in human response to uncontrollable circumstances.

Level 1: The strategic mind that tries to solve problems through analysis and intervention. This had been my entire approach to her autism: researching therapies, consulting experts, developing comprehensive strategies. It works for manageable challenges but becomes counterproductive with mysteries that resist solution.

Level 2: The development of equanimity, acceptance of what cannot be changed. I had gradually learned to find peace with her autism, to stop fighting against her natural way of being. This creates sustainability but can become passive.

Level 3: The recognition that the apparent separation between the one trying to change and what needs changing is itself an illusion. Enya had never lost this understanding. She didn't experience herself as separate from the flow of life, which is why she never developed the internal resistance that creates suffering.

What you seek to change, changes you.

This wasn't just philosophical insight – it was lived recognition. Every attempt to change her had changed me instead, gradually wearing away my assumptions about intelligence, communication, and authentic being until I could finally see what had been present all along.

Without the constant mental commentary that usually filled my consciousness, I could finally see what had been in front of me all along. Enya wasn't a problem to be solved. She was a teacher offering lessons in presence, authenticity, and forms of intelligence that operate outside conventional frameworks.

The rest of that week unfolded like a completely different kind of relationship. Instead of trying to engage her attention, I learned to follow where her attention was naturally drawn. Instead of attempting to teach her, I began to study what she was already demonstrating. Instead of trying to bring her into my world, I started to glimpse the world she inhabited.

By the end of the week, everything looked different. Not just my relationship with Enya, but my understanding of intelligence, communication, presence, and what it means to be fully human. The insights were so fundamental that they would continue to unfold for years, revealing new layers of meaning as I learned to integrate what I had discovered.

This week became the lens through which I would eventually reinterpret our entire journey together. I began to see that every year, every interaction, every moment of confusion or insight had been preparing me for this shift in understanding. She had been offering these teachings all along; I had simply been too preoccupied to receive them.

The electric shock of that week would continue to reverberate through every subsequent year of our relationship, revealing new dimensions of what I had learned about presence, acceptance, and the many forms that intelligence can take when it's not constrained by conventional expectations.

But for now, there was simply the astonishment of finally being awake in my daughter's presence, and the recognition that the most important education I would ever receive was happening in the space between a father's sleeping awareness and a child's uncompromising authenticity.

***

Amar B. Singh

What you seek to change, changes you!

What you seek to change, changes you
The world follows that, the mind too!

A stone stops water, flowing its course
The water finds a way, least resistance!
The stone doesn't go unchanged though
Gets eaten everyday by the water flow!

Totally eroded, relents eventually
The patient water flows; the stone becomes history!
The human mind sees this, ponders
Stopping water flow seems possible – with boulders!

We build dams!
Mountains of concrete!
The iron will, the great intellect!
Universal intelligence is patient though
Venting the water, is the priority now!

Eighteen Years with Enya

We vent, we irrigate, discuss and confer
Ego gets a boost – change courses of rivers
Encouraged, we learn how will works
We build dams, in our mind's murk!

The venting though, is difficult now
Mind transforms the chemistry, and how!

Small annoyances hit the dam, stay over
The flowing water now stale, changes nature…
Changes to frustration, converts to bother
Transforms eventually, into great anger!

We vent, as in the case of a dam
This water's different, irrespective of its name
We 'dammed' annoyance, we vented anger
My will has won and, I'm a loser!

I acted like the dam, acted like the stone
Never once I thought, left the water alone…
If I'm the water, can flow and dance
Go patiently down the path of least resistance!

My intellect but, serves my identity

Amar B. Singh

See myself separate from the eternity
We feel better, killing and losing,
Than flowing like water, being in sync…

Losing the 'ego', the ultimate fear
What's the world, when 'I' is not here…
So, we 'will', we 'dam, we 'vent', we lose…
Not a difficult choice though, when you see and choose!

5. The Hand That Knows

> Her touch arrived
> before my tears knew
> they were
> ready to fall.

Armed with the new awareness from that transformative week with Enya when she was eight, I began to notice things about her that I had been blind to for years. What I discovered was perhaps the most mysterious aspect of her intelligence – an ability to perceive emotional states that operated completely outside the frameworks of developmental psychology.

It started with what seemed like coincidences.

I would be sitting at my computer, working on a particularly frustrating project, feeling the early stirrings of irritation that I wasn't yet consciously aware of. Before the emotion had even fully formed in my mind, Enya would appear beside my chair and gently take my hand.

Not demanding anything. Not seeking attention. Just offering a kind of wordless comfort that seemed to arrive precisely when some part of me needed it most, even though I hadn't realized I needed anything at all.

At first, I attributed these moments to chance. Children have their own rhythms and reasons for seeking physical contact, after all. But as I began to pay closer attention – with the quality of awareness I had developed during our week together – I started to see a pattern that defied easy explanation.

She wasn't randomly affectionate. Her touches came with uncanny timing, always when I was approaching some internal threshold of stress, frustration, or emotional disturbance that I myself had not yet recognized.

One afternoon, I was reviewing some work emails that contained criticism about a project I had been leading. I was maintaining my professional composure, mentally formulating responses, not allowing myself to feel the sting of the feedback. But something in my nervous system was registering the threat to my sense of competence.

Before I had consciously acknowledged any emotional reaction, Enya walked over and placed her small hand on my forearm. The touch was gentle but unmistakably intentional – not the casual contact of a child seeking attention, but something that felt more like a therapeutic intervention.

"She grabbed your arm before you even got angry," my wife observed later that evening.

"I wasn't angry yet," I protested.

"Exactly. She felt it before you knew it."

I stared at my wife, trying to process this impossible statement. "That's not possible."

"Is it?" she asked quietly. "Watch tomorrow. See if she does it again."

The moment her hand made contact, I became aware of the tension I had been holding in my shoulders, the shallow breathing I hadn't noticed, the knot of anxiety forming in my stomach. She had somehow detected the physiological signs of stress before they had crossed the threshold into my conscious awareness.

How was this possible? According to every assessment she had ever received, her social awareness was limited. Her ability to read emotional cues was considered significantly delayed. Yet here she was, demonstrating a form of emotional intelligence that seemed to operate through channels I couldn't even identify, much less understand.

During a therapy session the following week, I mentioned this phenomenon to her occupational therapist.

"Some individuals with autism are highly sensitive to emotional states," the therapist explained. "They can pick up on changes in body language, breathing patterns, even subtle shifts in energy that neurotypical people might miss."

"She reads me better than I read myself," I admitted.

The therapist smiled. "Maybe that's a gift, not a deficit."

Her interventions weren't limited to detecting negative emotions. She seemed equally attuned to moments when I was experiencing genuine joy or contentment, though her responses to these states were different. Instead of offering comfort, she would often simply position herself nearby, as if she wanted to share in the positive energy without disrupting it.

I began to experiment with this phenomenon, testing whether her responses were truly connected to my internal states or if I was projecting patterns where none existed. I would deliberately call up different emotional memories while maintaining a neutral external appearance, and observe whether she showed any reaction.

The results were unsettling in their consistency. When I thought about work frustrations, relationship conflicts, or worries about her future, she would often appear within minutes, offering physical contact or simply positioning herself closer to me. When I focused on positive memories or feelings of gratitude, she seemed content to remain at whatever distance she had been before.

This wasn't the kind of emotional intelligence that psychology textbooks describe. She wasn't reading micro-expressions or interpreting verbal cues. She seemed to be directly perceiving the emotional field that surrounds human beings – the subtle energetic signatures that accompany different feeling states.

The most remarkable instance occurred during a period when I was dealing with some challenging decisions. I had been careful not to discuss these concerns in front of her, maintaining my usual demeanor while internally wrestling with anxiety about the future.

One evening, as I sat in the living room ostensibly reading a book but actually spiraling into worry about job security and family expenses, Enya suddenly appeared at my side. But instead of her usual gentle touch, she did something she had never done before: she climbed onto my lap, wrapped her arms around me, and held on with what felt like fierce protectiveness.

The embrace lasted for nearly ten minutes – an eternity in terms of her usual attention span for physical contact. It was as if she had sensed not just my current distress, but the depth and persistence of the worry I was carrying. Her response was proportioned to the intensity of what I was feeling, even though I had given no external sign of internal turmoil.

Later that night, I shared the experience with my wife over dinner.

"She felt things we haven't even felt yet," I mused.

"Like what?" my wife asked.

"Like the exact moment I stop being present with her," I realized. "And then she gently calls me back."

In that moment, I realized that she had been offering me emotional regulation support for years, but I had been too preoccupied to recognize it as such. What I had sometimes interpreted as clinginess or random affection was actually a sophisticated form of caregiving – her way of helping me maintain emotional equilibrium when my internal systems were becoming overwhelmed.

This discovery challenged everything I thought I understood about the relationship between cognitive development and emotional intelligence. Here was a child who couldn't speak, who struggled with conventional social interactions, who had been labeled as having significant developmental delays – yet she possessed a form of emotional awareness that surpassed anything I had encountered in typical adults.

Her ability to perceive emotional states seemed to operate in real-time, without the lag that characterizes conscious emotional recognition. While I might take minutes or even hours to fully acknowledge what I was feeling, she appeared to be receiving this information instantaneously.

But perhaps the most profound aspect of her emotional intelligence was how she used this information. She wasn't manipulative or self-serving in her responses to what she perceived. She seemed to operate from a place of pure compassion, offering comfort when it was needed without expecting anything in return.

***

My wife and I had been discussing having another child for years. It had first started as an answer to our fears about who would look after Enya after we are gone. But the reason we had been hesitant was different.

"I need to tell you something," my wife said one evening as we watched Enya watching TV and smiling while she tried to control the remote.

"I'm terrified about having another child."

"Because of the timing? The extra demands?"

"Because of the genetics." Her voice was barely above a whisper. "What if this baby is also autistic?"

The question hung between us like a challenge we weren't ready to face.

"The doctors said it's not necessarily hereditary," I offered weakly.

"The doctors don't know everything. Look at her," she gestured toward Enya, absorbed in her evening ritual. "They told us she was developing typically."

I could see her engineer's training at war with her mother's intuition. The medical knowledge that told her autism rates in siblings were elevated, competing with her heart that already loved the child growing inside her.

"That won't happen!" – my first reaction, followed by "It was the vaccine – we saw clearly. We will not go for vaccination this time!"

I realized it was my emotions speaking so looked at her – worried about something that hasn't happened and we had decided about this after years of discussions.

"Would it matter?" I asked carefully. "If the baby was also autistic?"

She was quiet for a long moment. "I don't know if I'm strong enough to do this twice. To fight the same battles, learn the same hard lessons, grieve the same dreams all over again."

"What if we didn't have to fight? What if we already know how to love differently?", I said and decided to go with the flow. We can't really fight the universe.

***

The pregnancy announcement came when Enya was eight, during one of our most challenging periods with her development. My wife worried about managing two children when one required such intensive attention. I worried about how a sibling might affect Enya's routines.

"What if the baby cries and disrupts her sleep?" my wife asked during one of our late-night conversations.

"What if she doesn't understand why we're giving attention to someone else?" I added.

We couldn't have predicted that the baby growing in my wife's womb would become Enya's greatest advocate, translator, and protector.

***

Aaryaveer arrived, a wiggly, vocal bundle of typical development that created an immediate contrast in our household. Where Enya moved with careful deliberation, he was chaos in motion. Where she required predictable routines, he thrived on variety and surprise.

But something beautiful happened in those early months. Enya, who had always been sensitive to disruption, seemed to understand that this small human belonged to our family. She would position herself near his crib during his crying episodes, not covering her ears as she did with other unexpected sounds, but sitting quietly as if keeping watch.

When he began crawling towards her, she would gently redirect him toward his own things – not with irritation, but with the patience of someone who understood he was still learning the rules.

This wasn't learned behavior in any conventional sense. No one had taught her how to respond with such precision and care. It appeared to be an innate capacity that had developed outside the normal channels of social learning.

Her emotional interventions never felt intrusive or inappropriate. She seemed to have an intuitive understanding of when to offer physical comfort, when to simply be present, and when to maintain distance. This discriminating awareness suggested a level of social intelligence that existed independently of her ability to engage in conventional social interactions.

I began to wonder whether her apparent social difficulties were actually the result of being overwhelmed by too much emotional information rather than too little. Perhaps she was receiving such a rich stream of emotional data from the people around her that conventional social interactions felt chaotic and overwhelming.

If she could perceive the emotional states of everyone in a room simultaneously, if she was constantly aware of the anxieties, frustrations, and hidden feelings that adults work so hard to conceal, then her tendency to retreat into stimming or what can be called her own shell of activities might be a form of self-protection rather than social avoidance.

This realization reframed my understanding of her entire social presentation. What looked like withdrawal might actually be wisdom – the recognition that most human social interaction is layered with emotional complexity that requires careful navigation.

Her hand knew things that my mind couldn't grasp. Her touch arrived with information that my cognitive awareness hadn't yet processed. She was demonstrating forms of intelligence that operated outside the categories we use to measure and understand human development.

The hand that knows became my introduction to the possibility that consciousness itself might operate according to principles that our current models of psychology and neurology don't adequately explain. That intelligence might include capacities that emerge when the usual filters of mental analysis are bypassed or underdeveloped.

She was teaching me that some of the most important human capabilities – empathy, emotional awareness, the ability to offer comfort at precisely the right moment – might not depend on language, cognitive sophistication, or conventional social learning at all.

They might depend on something more direct, more immediate, more mysterious – the kind of knowing that arrives through touch before thought, through presence before analysis, through a form of intelligence that recognizes what is needed without having to figure out why.

The Meltdown Mirror

The meltdown happened on a Tuesday evening at the grocery store, in full view of at least twenty other shoppers. At the time, I experienced it as one of those parenting moments you hope will never come – a public display of what looked like complete loss of control that left me feeling helpless, embarrassed, and deeply concerned about Enya's wellbeing.

It would take me months to understand that she had actually given me one of the most important teachings about emotional authenticity I would ever receive.

We had started the shopping trip in good spirits. Enya seemed calm and content, moving through the store with her usual methodical approach to new environments. She was drawn to the produce section, fascinated by the precise arrangements of fruits and vegetables, the way colors were organized, the tactile variety of different textures.

I was feeling proud of how smoothly things were going. Here we were, father and daughter, navigating a complex public space together without any of the difficulties that had characterized our early outings. I was congratulating myself on how much progress we had both made in learning to read each other's cues and needs.

But I wasn't paying close enough attention to the subtle signs that something was building beneath the surface of her apparent calm. The slight increase in her pace as we moved through the aisles. The way her fingers began to seek out textures more urgently. The almost imperceptible tension that was gathering in her shoulders.

Looking back with the awareness I've developed since then, I can see that she was managing an increasing level of sensory overwhelm – the fluorescent lights, the background noise of other shoppers, the visual complexity of thousands of products arranged in overwhelming abundance. She was working hard to maintain her equilibrium in an environment that was pushing her nervous system toward its limits.

The triggers were absurdly insignificant for others: shining lights, colorful clothes, and then a shopping cart that someone pushed too close to her, creating a sudden metallic scraping sound as its wheels caught on something. For most people, this would have been a minor annoyance, easily dismissed. For Enya, in her already heightened state of sensory processing, it was the final input that pushed her system beyond its capacity to cope.

What followed looked like chaos but was actually a completely authentic expression of nervous system overwhelm.

She shut down to the world, looked at me but helplessly started raising her voice as if listening to her own self to forget everything around – hands clasping each other, body curled into a protective position. The sounds she made weren't quite crying – they were more like vocalizations of pure distress, expressions of sensation that had become unbearable. Her whole body was communicating: Too much. Can't process. Need safety.

In the moment, I felt the familiar surge of emotions that accompany public parenting challenges: embarrassment at the attention we were drawing, concern for her distress, frustration at my inability to immediately fix the situation, and a kind of protective anger at the judgmental looks I imagined we were receiving.

A store clerk approached, her face showing the mixture of concern and irritation that retail workers develop for disruptions to their environment.

"Sir, what happened? Your daughter is disturbing other customers," she said. I felt rage building in my chest before I could even think. "She's overwhelmed. We're leaving."

But something from that transformative week with Enya kicked in. Instead of trying to rush her through the episode or manage the social discomfort, I found myself simply standing beside her in the grocery store, offering my presence without trying to change what was happening.

As I stood there, watching her move through the storm of sensation and emotion, I began to see something I had never noticed before. Her response was completely honest. There was no performance in it, no manipulation, no hidden agenda. She was simply expressing exactly what she was experiencing in the moment, without any of the filters that adults use to make their emotional states socially acceptable.

The other shoppers' reactions were mixed. Some looked uncomfortable, clearly wanting to move past the scene as quickly as possible. Others showed genuine concern, asking if there was anything they could do to help. A few seemed to understand intuitively that this was simply a child processing something difficult and that the best response was patient acceptance.

But I was struck by how much more authentic the entire situation felt than the polite facades that characterize most public interactions. Her expression of distress was cutting through the usual social pretense, creating a moment of real human vulnerability in a space that's normally defined by commercial efficiency and emotional suppression.

After about ten minutes, the storm began to pass. Her breathing gradually deepened, her body started to relax, her hands slowly moved away from her ears. She remained static for another few minutes, seeming to test whether the environment had become manageable again.

When she finally stopped, there was something different in her demeanor. Not shame or embarrassment about what had just happened, but a kind of clarity that comes after authentic emotional expression. She had felt something difficult, expressed it completely, and moved through it to a state of renewed equilibrium.

I, on the other hand, was discovering layers of my own emotional response that I hadn't initially recognized. Beneath the embarrassment and concern, I was actually feeling something like envy. When was the last time I had allowed myself to express overwhelm so completely? When had I last honored my own nervous system's signals instead of powering through discomfort in service of social expectations?

Her meltdown was serving as a mirror, reflecting back to me the ways I had learned to suppress and manage my own emotional responses. I had become so skilled at maintaining social composure that I had lost touch with the authentic signals my body was constantly sending about stress, overwhelm, and the need for rest or change.

The recognition that my surface calm often concealed the same emotional bubbles that Enya expressed so directly. The difference was that she allowed them to surface and release, while I tried to manage them at the bottom of the lake, where they accumulated and eventually demanded explosive expression.

We finished our shopping with a different quality of attention. I found myself much more sensitive to the sensory complexity of the environment we were navigating, more aware of the cumulative impact of fluorescent lights, background noise, and visual overwhelm. Her meltdown had opened my perception to experiences that I had learned to tune out but that were constantly affecting both of us.

In the car afterward, my wife looked at me with curiosity. "You were angrier than she was."

"She can't defend herself," I protested.

"Can't she? Did you see how calmly she handled it once she got what she needed?"

I realized she was right. While I had wanted to shout at someone for their lack of understanding, Enya had simply expressed her distress, received the space she needed, and returned to equilibrium. No blame, no resentment, no story about how unfair the world was.

"Who's having the meltdown now?" my wife asked gently.

That evening, as I sat on Enya's bed during our usual bedtime routine, I found myself apologizing.

"I'm sorry you saw Papa get so angry today," I said quietly.

She looked at me with those steady eyes and gently touched my hand – her universal gesture of comfort.

"You're not the one with the problem, are you? I am," I said, more to myself than to her.

I realized that I couldn't remember the last time I had allowed myself such authentic emotional expression. When I felt overwhelmed, I suppressed it. When I was angry, I found socially appropriate ways to channel it. When I was afraid or confused, I masked these feelings behind competence and control.

But here was my daughter, demonstrating what it looked like to feel something completely and express it without shame or apology. Her meltdown wasn't a failure of emotional regulation – it was a masterclass in emotional honesty.

That evening, I called a friend who had asked how I handled the public stares that came with having a visibly different child.

"Enya handles them better than I do," I found myself saying.

"What do you mean?" he asked.

"She doesn't take them personally. She just exists. I'm the one who gets defensive."

What I was slowly understanding was that her emotional storms had always served this function – not just as expressions of her own overwhelm, but as invitations for me to examine my own relationship with authentic feeling.

When she had meltdowns at home, I would often feel my own stress levels rising, my own need to control the situation, my own discomfort with emotional intensity. But these responses revealed more about my own emotional suppression than about her emotional dysfunction.

Her willingness to feel everything completely, to express it authentically, and to move through it without shame was actually demonstrating a form of emotional intelligence that most adults have lost. She wasn't broken or dysregulated – she was emotionally honest in ways that challenged the entire social contract around acceptable feeling and expression.

I began to see that my attempts to help her develop "better emotional regulation" were actually attempts to teach her the same suppression strategies that had disconnected me from my own authentic emotional experience. What if the goal wasn't to help her manage her feelings more like an adult, but to help me learn to feel more like a child?

The meltdown mirror showed me that emotional authenticity and social functioning don't have to be mutually exclusive. It's possible to honor genuine emotional responses while also developing skills for navigating complex social environments. But the starting point has to be acceptance of what is actually being felt, not suppression in service of what looks socially appropriate.

Her storms were teaching me that there's a difference between emotional regulation and emotional suppression. True regulation includes the ability to feel completely, express authentically, and move through difficult emotions to a state of genuine resolution. Suppression just pushes emotions underground where they create ongoing tension and disconnection.

That grocery store meltdown became a turning point in how I understood not just her emotional responses, but emotions themselves. She was demonstrating that feelings are meant to be felt completely, expressed authentically, and released naturally – not managed, controlled, or performed according to social expectations.

The mirror she held up showed me how much emotional vitality I had sacrificed in the name of adult competence and social acceptability. Her meltdowns weren't problems to be solved – they were teachings about the difference between emotional authenticity and emotional performance.

And slowly, very slowly, I began to learn.

Amar B. Singh

The Deep Lake

Happy and peaceful, like a still lake
The feelings were pleasant, not fake!

Could see, with some focus, the upcoming bubbles
Small, harmless and yet, caused big ripples

The lake, still no more, its surface distraught
Anger had taken over, too late to be fought!

Noticed nevertheless, memorized and filed
Next time, with focus, the bubble, will be killed!

Risky it seemed, the lake was big
Too many bubbles moving up, for me to see!

Needs to be corrected at source, I thought
Jumped into the lake, skipped the boat!

Absolutely different form the surface, was the bottom
Very small bubbles, many in formation…

The source but, was my own waste decaying
Was wrong all this while, am rid of nothing!

My tree leaving seeds, seeds creating trees back…
Action made sense not at the bottom, but at the top!

Don't throw the decay, don't suppress the me
Don't control the bubble, focus and 'see'!

For once the seed is destroyed, so goes the tree
Understand the 'me', live consciously!

The lake is deep, dark, quite unexplorable!
Attention can only solve the symptom – the bubble!

This 'action' from the bottom of the lake
Undone only when I realize the 'me' fake!

Identifying myself as my body and mind,
Continues to create bubbles (& ripples), of all kinds!

Fear, jealousy, attachment, pain & sorrow,
Kill me every day – yesterday, today and tomorrow!

Amar B. Singh

But, once, having seen who I really am
    The seeds die, the tree begone!

Once again, the lake, beautiful and still,
    No time, no space, no illusion of will!

I lie in peace, God smiles from the sky
He lives in me, no questions, no 'made me why'!

6. Intelligence in Disguise

She walks out with me to the car at 9:30 AM sharp. Before that, she is ready and waiting, her green uniform already carefully selected. She doesn't run to the gate like other children might, but she moves with purpose, her shy smile directed downward as she takes measured steps toward her day.

At the Soham foundation, where she spends her school time, she navigates the space like someone who belongs. Not because she follows schedules or completes tasks, but because she has claimed this territory as hers. She knows which activities call to her – the sensory training with its gentle lights, the music corner where melodies wash over everything else. The staff has learned to read her rhythm: when she wants to engage, when she needs space, when the day has offered enough.

I watch her during pickup, noticing how she chooses her moments. She doesn't perform for approval or resist for attention. She simply is – present in her own way, engaging on her own terms. When she's ready to leave, she takes my hand and leads me towards the car. No words needed, no negotiation required.

The car ride home is when her true preferences emerge most clearly. Before I can even start the engine, she's reaching for my hand, guiding it toward the air conditioning controls. Too cold – she moves my fingers to warm it up. The music comes next, her soft yet firm fingers directing mine through the track change controls on the car steering, until she finds the melody that matches her internal rhythm. Only then does she settle back, positioning herself at the window, ready to receive whatever the journey offers.

Those early years, I had measured progress in therapist reports and development milestones. I waited for breakthroughs that looked like other children's victories – first words spoken clearly, social games played correctly, skills mastered in recognizable ways. The foundation wasn't failing her, but I was failing to see what success looked like in her world.

Her foundation experience wasn't about catching up to typical development. It was about honoring her natural way of being while giving her tools to navigate a world designed for others. She didn't need to be fixed; she needed space to be herself and grow into her own fullness.

Watching her guide my hand to the car controls, I began to understand a different kind of intelligence at work. She knew exactly what she wanted and exactly how to get it. She understood cause and effect, human psychology, and environmental control better than most adults. But she did it all without words, without explanations, without performing competence in ways others expected.

I started recognizing her sophistication everywhere: how she timed her requests perfectly, how she used touch and gesture more effectively than most people use language, how she created the conditions for her own comfort and joy. The foundation became a place where these gifts could flourish rather than a place where deficits were addressed.

Education isn't about making children fit into predetermined molds – it's about creating environments where each child's natural intelligence can emerge and develop. Enya taught me that progress doesn't always look like meeting benchmarks or mastering skills in expected ways.

Her form of learning is relational, experiential, sensory. She absorbs environments, understands people, and solves problems through embodied intelligence that operates below the level of conscious thought.

Eighteen Years with Enya

***

But it was her choices at home – in her own territory, with her own rhythm – where I would discover the true depth of her intelligence. The foundation had given her tools, but home was where she wielded them with masterful precision.

The irony was so stark it felt like the universe was playing an elaborate joke on me. There I was, spending my days working on an artificial intelligence paper – trying to understand how machines can recognize patterns, process information, and make intelligent decisions – while completely failing to recognize the sophisticated intelligence that was operating right beside me in my own home.

The earlier school evaluations had painted a consistent picture of limitation. The feedback was about her inability to follow multi-step verbal instructions was documented as evidence of processing difficulties. Her resistance to traditional learning activities was interpreted as lack of motivation or comprehension.

During a parent-teacher conference, her teacher expressed concern about Enya's performance.

"She is very low on the cognitive assessment," the teacher explained, showing us her methods.

"Watch her navigate our house in complete darkness," I countered, thinking of how she moved through familiar spaces with remarkable spatial awareness.

"That's spatial intelligence, not academic," the teacher replied dismissively.

"Who decided academic intelligence is the only kind that counts?" I asked, feeling frustration rise in my chest.

But the more time I spent actually observing her – with the quality of attention I had developed during that transformative week

— the more I began to see forms of intelligence that had no place in any assessment I was familiar with.

During a doctor's appointment, when the physician noted her developmental delays, I tried to convey what I was seeing at home.

"Her verbal responses suggest developmental delays," the doctor observed.

"Her non-verbal responses suggest she understands everything," I replied.

"We can only measure what we can test," he said with the finality that medical professionals use to end challenging conversations.

"Then maybe your tests are incomplete," I suggested.

At home, my wife and I would often marvel at demonstrations of intelligence that didn't fit any category we understood.

"She was sitting in the other room and heard you speak the words "walking outside" and is already standing here smiling", my wife observed one evening.

"But can't answer 'What's your name?'" I replied, highlighting the contradiction that defined our daily experience with her.

"Maybe the question is irrelevant to her," my wife suggested.

"Maybe intelligence has nothing to do with answering our questions," I realized, starting to grasp something fundamental about different forms of knowing.

We were programming computers to recognize limited sets of patterns, to process information according to predetermined algorithms, to make decisions based on statistical probabilities.

But Enya was demonstrating forms of intelligence that seemed to operate through direct perception, intuitive understanding, and processing methods that bypassed the sequential logic that characterizes both human reasoning and computer programming.

Her response to music provided another window into intelligence that didn't fit conventional categories. While she couldn't demonstrate musical knowledge through traditional means like singing songs, playing instruments, following written notation, she had developed an extraordinarily sophisticated relationship with rhythm, tone, and harmonic structure.

She could predict when a song was about to end, not by counting measures or following lyrical patterns, but through some direct apprehension of musical architecture. She would begin moving toward the door just before the final notes of a piece she had never heard before, as if she could sense the approaching resolution.

When I played classical music while working, she would position herself in different parts of the room depending on the piece. Complex, layered compositions seemed to draw her to the center of the space, while simpler melodies would find her at the periphery. I began to suspect she was navigating some kind of acoustic map that was invisible to me but perfectly clear to her.

The educational system had no framework for recognizing this as intelligence. There were no tests for spatial-musical integration, no assessments for environmental navigation through non-verbal pattern recognition, no categories for intelligence that operated through direct sensory engagement rather than symbolic processing.

Her memory capabilities revealed similar contradictions. She couldn't of course, demonstrate retention of information through conventional recall methods – answering questions about stories, repeating sequences of instructions, or completing memory-based academic tasks.

But she had developed her own memory – refusing to eat what she hadn't liked earlier if served to her again after weeks. Similarly, she developed what seemed like photographic memory for certain types of environmental details. She could lead us to specific shops we had visited months earlier, remembering not just the route but particular visual markers along the way. She could identify when objects in familiar spaces had been moved, even when the changes were subtle enough that I hadn't noticed them.

This form of memory wasn't organized around the verbal categories that characterize most human learning. She wasn't remembering words, concepts, or stories. She was encoding direct sensory experiences in ways that allowed perfect reconstruction of spatial and temporal relationships.

During one of my internal reflections, watching her navigate these different forms of intelligence, I found myself thinking: "We're measuring her intelligence by our standards. But what if her intelligence operates on frequencies we can't even detect?"

When I tried to understand how this worked by asking her to demonstrate or explain, I would encounter the same frustration I had seen with her spatial arrangements. The intelligence she was using operated outside the frameworks that depend on verbal communication or symbolic representation.

Her problem-solving abilities followed similar patterns. She couldn't work through logical puzzles that required step-by-step reasoning or verbal analysis. But she could solve mechanical problems through what appeared to be immediate understanding of how physical systems worked.

I watched her figure out how to operate complex door mechanisms, not through trial and error or following instructions, but through some direct apprehension of the relationships between different components. She seemed to see how things worked rather than thinking her way through their operation.

The more I observed these capabilities, the more I began to question the entire foundation of how we measure and understand intelligence. The assessments that labeled her as cognitively delayed were measuring a very specific type of intelligence – one that operates through language, symbolic reasoning, and sequential processing.

But they were completely blind to forms of intelligence that operate through direct perception, spatial integration, pattern recognition that bypasses conscious analysis, and problem-solving that works through immediate understanding rather than step-by-step reasoning.

I realized that our educational systems were designed around the assumption that there is essentially one type of intelligence – the kind that can be measured through verbal and mathematical assessments, demonstrated through linear thinking, and developed through instruction that proceeds from simple to complex in predetermined sequences.

But Enya was demonstrating that intelligence might be far more diverse than our institutions recognize. That there might be forms of knowing that operate according to completely different principles than the ones our schools are designed to support.

The breakthrough moment came when I stopped trying to understand her intelligence through the categories I was familiar with and started simply observing what she could actually do. When I let go of expectations based on developmental norms and standardized assessments, I could see capabilities that were far more sophisticated than anything being measured in her evaluations.

She wasn't lacking intelligence – she was demonstrating forms of intelligence that our frameworks couldn't recognize, much less support or develop.

Her struggles weren't evidence of cognitive limitation. They were evidence of a profound mismatch between her natural learning style and the narrow range of intelligence that education is designed to cultivate.

By the end of her eleventh year, I had stopped seeing her academic difficulties as problems to be solved and started seeing them as evidence that intelligence itself might be far more mysterious and diverse than any of our current models suggest.

She was teaching me that there might be forms of natural intelligence that operate according to principles we don't yet understand – intelligence that works through direct perception rather than analysis, through immediate understanding rather than sequential reasoning, through integration rather than compartmentalization.

And perhaps most importantly, she was showing me that some of the most sophisticated forms of intelligence might be invisible to assessment tools that can only measure what they're designed to recognize.

The magic I couldn't understand was actually the future of intelligence itself – naturalistic, integrative, immediate, and far more sophisticated than anything we were trying to create artificially.

***

Eighteen Years with Enya

The Intelligence of Choices

Home at 2 PM, and Enya has her sequence. The iPad appears in her hands like magic – she knows exactly where I keep it, exactly how to navigate to her music. YouTube opens to her curated collection of melodies, songs that seem chosen by some inner algorithm I can't decode. Sometimes it's party songs, at times piano, sometimes Bollywood melodies, sometimes simple children's songs that she's loved for years. But never random, never chaotic – always purposeful.

I have tried to understand her selection process. There's no pattern I can name, yet there's deep consistency in what calls to her. She'll skip past dozens of songs with the same focused attention a scholar brings to research, until she finds the one that matches whatever internal state she's seeking to create or maintain.

When she tires of the iPad, she migrates to the television, again with precise intent. Not channel surfing like the rest of us, but seeking specific content that serves specific needs. Music videos, usually, but with visual elements that complement the audio – colors, movements, rhythms that create a complete sensory experience. What really baffled me for a significant time, is when she started a song and then went back on the remote and restarted it and this was done at least for the next half an hour. I realized after a while that she like how the music starts – the first few notes…

The evening walk is non-negotiable, but the route is always hers to choose. She'll start in one direction, then pause, considering. Sometimes she'll change course entirely, leading us down paths I wouldn't have chosen. She reads the environment in ways I'm only beginning to appreciate. Her route selection feels random until you realize she's creating a perfect sensory journey, calibrating the day's inputs and outputs with mathematical precision.

During her time at home, I watch her remove items that don't belong. Not organizing them into neat patterns, but simply making them disappear. A pen goes into the drawer, papers slide under the sofa, anything that disrupts her visual field gets relocated to invisible places. She's not cleaning – she's curating, creating an environment that allows her nervous system to settle.

***

For years, I had looked for her intelligence in the wrong places. I expected it to show up in language, in academics, in social performances that looked like everyone else's demonstrations of capability. I missed the profound sophistication of her environmental management, her sensory wisdom, her intuitive understanding of her own needs.

She doesn't organize things systematically because she doesn't think systematically – she thinks holistically. Rather than imposing order through categories and rules, she creates harmony by removing discord. It's a more elegant solution: instead of arranging complexity, simply eliminate what doesn't serve.

Her choice-making operates at a level that bypasses the analytical mind entirely. She doesn't deliberate or second-guess or seek approval. She knows what she wants with a clarity that makes most adult decision-making look clumsy by comparison. She's never chosen something she didn't actually want, never acted against her own best interests, never betrayed her authentic preferences for social acceptance.

Watching her navigate her day with such precision, I realized I was witnessing a form of intelligence that our culture barely recognizes. She's not thinking her way through problems – she's embodying solutions. She's not analyzing her environment – she's harmonizing with it.

***

Intelligence comes in forms we don't measure, operating through channels we don't recognize. Enya's way of knowing is immediate, embodied, and utterly practical. She solves problems by changing conditions rather than changing thoughts.

Her intelligence is ecological – she understands herself as part of systems and creates the conditions for her own flourishing without needing to explain or justify her methods to anyone.

The shift in my father's understanding happened gradually, so slowly I almost missed it.

During one visit, I found him sitting quietly with Enya as she arranged her collections of small objects. He wasn't trying to engage her or redirect her activity. He was simply – present, and watching.

"She has her own wisdom," he said without looking up from her careful sorting.

"What do you mean?"

"The astrologers, the healers, the gemstones - I was trying to fix something that wasn't broken." He picked up one of her sorted stones, examined it, then placed it back exactly where she had positioned it. "She already knows how to find peace. I was the one who needed teaching."

This was perhaps the most profound statement I had ever heard him make about Enya. Not about her deficits or her karmic challenges, but about her inherent wisdom.

"The prayers weren't for her," he continued. "They were for me. To help me see clearly."

**

When Aaryaveer's first words came right on schedule, my wife's relief was almost palpable. But what surprised both of us was the guilt that followed.

"I feel terrible," she confided one evening as we watched our verbal, socially engaged toddler chatter away. "I was so grateful he was talking, and then I felt like I was betraying Enya."

"How so?"

"Like I was saying her way wasn't good enough. Like I was relieved he was 'normal' when she's perfect exactly as she is."

This tension would follow us for months - the joy of typical development shadowed by the recognition that we had unconsciously been mourning Enya's different path even while learning to celebrate it.

"Maybe," I suggested, watching Aaryaveer babble to his sister who listened with patient attention, "we needed him to be typical so we could finally stop worrying about normal and just appreciate authentic."

***

It's Tuesday afternoon, and I'm reading in the living room when Enya appears at my elbow. Not just appears – arrives with intention. She takes my hand in both of hers, not gently, but with the kind of purposeful grip that says attention required. She shakes it once, twice, just enough to pull me fully into the present moment.

Our eyes meet. Direct. Unwavering. The kind of eye contact that cuts through all the adult noise in my head – the emails, the deadlines, the mental chatter. In that gaze, there's complete clarity about what's happening: this is not a casual interaction.

"Walking," she says, stretching the word like taffy, making it last twice as long as necessary. "Walk-ing." Her hands release mine to form the sign - two fingers on her t-shirt moving down in a curvature – while her voice carries the elongated vowels that somehow convey not just the word, but the depth of wanting behind it.

She doesn't stop there. Her free hand gestures toward the front door, then returns to tug at my shirt sleeve. The sequence is precise, orchestrated: word + sign + voice modulation + physical guidance + visual anchoring. It's a full-body conversation happening in thirty seconds.

"Shoes," she adds, pointing toward the urgency of the previous request, her voice still carrying that stretched importance.

I close my book. How could I not? She's just delivered a masterpiece of communication that engaged every sense I have. My hands felt her urgency, my eyes received her direct message, my ears heard both the word and the emotional undertone, my body understood the physical direction she wanted me to move.

At the institute and at home, she had worked with word cards, matching pictures to letters, slowly building what the educators call "functional communication." The progress charts show small increments – five new word recognitions this month, improved picture-to-word matching. But here in our living room, she's demonstrating something far more sophisticated.

When she hears me mention "walk" to my wife from across the house, Enya appears within seconds, already signing and smiling, already saying "shoes, walking, outside" with that anticipatory joy that tells me she's been listening, processing, planning. She understands not just words, but timing, context, social cues.

The "chips" request last week was even more elaborate. She led me to the kitchen, opened the refrigerator door, pointed to the specific bag, then looked back at me with raised eyebrows – a clear question mark. When I didn't immediately respond, she repeated the sequence: "Chips," with the sign, pointing again, the eyebrow inquiry. When I finally reached for the bag, her smile bloomed like sunrise.

This isn't someone trapped by language barriers. This is someone who has created her own elegant solution to the bridge between inner experience and outer expression.

For years, I carried a quiet grief about Enya's communication. Not about her specifically, but about what I assumed she couldn't access – the easy flow of conversation, the casual exchange of ideas, the simple pleasure of saying exactly what you mean when you mean it.

I watched other children her age chattering effortlessly, their words tumbling over each other in streams of consciousness, and I felt the weight of everything I imagined she couldn't share. The stories locked inside her. The observations she couldn't voice. The connection I feared we might never have.

I was seeing lack where there was actually innovation.

What I mistook for limitation was Enya developing a communication system far more sophisticated than what most adults use. While we rely primarily on words – often imprecise, easily misunderstood words – she created a full-spectrum language that makes misunderstanding nearly impossible.

When she wants something, I don't just hear it, I feel it, see it, experience it. Her urgency becomes my urgency through the pressure of her grip. Her joy becomes visible in her posture, her facial expressions, her whole-body enthusiasm. Her meaning arrives through multiple channels simultaneously, creating a richness of communication that most verbal exchanges lack.

I think about my own conversations with other adults. How often do we actually connect? How much gets lost in translation, even when we're speaking the same language? How many times do

I say "fine" when I mean something else entirely, or ask "how are you?" without really wanting to know?

Enya doesn't do small talk. Every communication has purpose, intention, clarity. When she looks at me, she's fully present. When she speaks, it's because something matters enough to warrant the effort. When she combines her signs with sounds with physical guidance, she's creating a moment of complete understanding between us.

She rarely seems frustrated now in the way she did as a younger child, when the gap between her inner experience and her ability to express it felt wider. She's found her bridge, and it's more beautiful than anything I could have imagined.

Language isn't binary – verbal or silent, fluent or impaired, normal or alternative. Enya created a third way: a communication system that engages body, voice, signs, timing, emotional resonance, anticipatory care, and real-time social negotiation all at once. What we call "limited" communication is actually enhanced communication – impossible to misunderstand because it uses every channel available.

She didn't develop around a disability; she developed toward a more complete form of human connection. Her communication includes not just her needs, but mine. Not just the present moment, but anticipation of what's coming. Not just expression, but emotional regulation and social awareness working simultaneously.

While we adults often hide behind words that say little and mean less, Enya created a language of pure intention where every gesture carries meaning, every glance negotiates understanding, and every moment of connection builds trust.

That look in her eyes when her joy overflows public boundaries – apologetic yet unapologetic, aware yet authentic – is more sophisticated emotional communication than most adults achieve even with thousands of words.

This evening, as I watch her navigate her after-dinner routine with the same precise attention she brings to all her communications, I'm struck by how the institutional focus on deficits misses the innovations she's actually developing.

The progress they measure – words acquired, symbols recognized, responses improved – represents only a fraction of the communication mastery she's demonstrating. What they can't measure is the quality of connection she creates, the depth of understanding she ensures, the reliability of the bridge she's built between her inner experience and the world's ability to receive it.

Progress, I'm learning, isn't always about becoming more like everyone else. Sometimes it's about becoming more perfectly yourself while finding ways to share that perfection with those who need to learn how to see.

***

The Pursuit of Intelligence

Late afternoon yesterday

She touched my hand

Seemed to say, "Hey"

"I want something I can't describe to you"

"Sincerely hoping you understand, what I don't say now"

I moved; the paper rustled

She looked at me

Her eyes feeling she had me hassled

Reassured her, paid all my attention

Offered her words, guessing all she could've wanted…

She tried hard for another minute

I still had no clue but.

Continued working on the value proposition

Noticed it was on 'artificial intelligence'

What kind of intelligence, I wondered?

When my world was getting squandered…

Amar B. Singh

For lack of natural intelligence, nothing else,
Making the machine prudent, but not the self!

Machine learning and fuzzy logic
While I don't understand my kid's magic
Pursuing intellect, calling it intelligence…
Life stares at me, blank in the face!

PART III: THE DEEPENING

Amar B. Singh

Seizure

The electrical activity, in the brain surged
She stood, head shaking, her face was quivered!

Rushed in her mom,
The worst she feared,
Calmed herself down,
Applied protocol standard

The worship of Gods,
Was the day of victory!
Nine nights of Navratri done,
It was Vijay Dashami!

Truth, the 'Dharma', wins
Can't be otherwise…
The choice of the day so,
Took me by surprise!

Science sees too little,

Much wider is life's scope…

What does one do but?
Except for faith & hope…

What I reap, it's fair, that I sow,
How do I explain what she goes through, though!

Desperate, I turn to my books
Don't find answers, have looked all nooks!
Picked up words – 'absence' & 'myoclonic'
No use though in this experience cyclonic…

'Prarabdha', I won't take for an answer!
Can explain some years, not her life forever?

And yet, what can I do, but to God, mention,
In me, are you, help me – show me the dimension…?

7. The Seizure – Dense Helplessness

> When her brain became electric storm,
> I learned that love
> is what remains
> when understanding fails.

December 2018. We had just returned from Jim Corbett National Park, and for the first time in years, I felt genuine optimism about Enya's development. Something about being in the jungle had awakened a different quality of engagement in her – more alert, more responsive, more present in ways that seemed to suggest new possibilities emerging as she entered her teenage years.

She had been fascinated by the natural environment in ways that went beyond her usual sensory interests. The sounds of birds, the patterns of light through trees, the complex ecosystems of the forest seemed to activate forms of awareness that I had never seen before. She appeared more connected, more communicative, more alive to the world around her.

For months leading up to that trip, we had been cautiously hopeful that adolescence might bring the developmental breakthrough that had eluded us throughout her childhood. Some parents reported that their autistic children showed significant progress during the teenage years – new forms of communication, increased social awareness, even the emergence of speech in children who had been non-verbal for years.

The seizure came without warning on a December morning, One moment she was sitting peacefully in the living room, and the next moment something I had never witnessed before was happening to her body.

The first thing I noticed was her eyes. They rolled upward in a way that looked completely unnatural, showing mostly white, as if she was looking at something invisible above her head.

My wife appeared instantly. I could see the terror in her eyes. She moved Enya away from anything that could cause injury, and placed a pillow under her head. But we both knew we were witnessing something far beyond our ability to manage or understand.

In the emergency room, the questions came rapid-fire: "Has this happened before?" the doctor asked.

"Never. She was just... sitting there, and then..." I struggled to find words for what we had witnessed.

"Will this happen again?" my wife asked.

"We don't know," came the response that would become achingly familiar.

The three words I hate most: "We don't know." After years of seeking understanding, developing frameworks, learning to decode her mysteries, we were suddenly in territory where expertise offered no comfort and experience provided no guidance.

At the hospital, they put her on a ventilator because none of us – not the doctors, not the nurses, not my wife with her medical training – had immediately recognized what was happening as a seizure. We had only seen her eyes rolling upward and her body convulsing, symptoms that could indicate any number of medical emergencies.

Lying in that hospital bed, connected to machines that monitored brain activity I couldn't interpret, she looked smaller and more vulnerable than I had ever seen her. The confidence and engagement she had shown just days earlier in the natural environment of Jim Corbett seemed like it belonged to a different person, a different life.

The neurologist explained seizure types and prescribed anti-epileptic medications with the careful precision of someone who understood the mechanisms but couldn't explain the meaning. "Sometimes these things just emerge during adolescence," he said. "Brain development can trigger seizure activity in children who have never had them before."

But his explanations felt hollow against the weight of what we had experienced. This wasn't just a medical event – it was an encounter with the fundamental mystery of consciousness itself, the recognition that the person we loved could be overtaken by electrical storms that had nothing to do with her will, her intelligence, or her essential being.

In the hospital waiting room, my wife voiced what we were both feeling: "I keep thinking I should have seen it coming."

"How could you? I was right there too," I replied, though I was plagued by the same impossible guilt.

"What if this changes everything?" she whispered.

"Everything already changed. We just didn't know it yet."

Later, sitting beside her bed during the long nights of monitoring, I found myself speaking to her unconscious form: "I thought I understood helplessness before. I was wrong. All my plans, all my strategies... none of it matters now, does it?"

When I called my mother to update her on Enya's condition, her voice carried the weight of a grandmother's particular fear.

"How is she?" my mother asked.

"Stable. Whatever that means," I said.

"And how are you?"

"Learning that some things are completely beyond my control."

The seizures continued sporadically over the following months, each one a reminder of how little control we actually had over the fundamental conditions of our lives. The medications helped reduce their frequency, but they also seemed to dull some of the brightness that had been emerging in her personality.

What disturbed me most wasn't the medical challenge of managing a seizure disorder – it was the recognition that all the progress we thought we had made in understanding her, all the insights I had gained about her intelligence and capabilities, could be swept away by neurological events that had nothing to do with her essential nature.

The seizures introduced a different kind of helplessness than anything we had experienced before. With her autism, I had at least been able to develop frameworks for understanding her behavior, theories about her intelligence, approaches to supporting her development. But seizures existed in a realm beyond understanding or intervention.

I realized that I had been unconsciously building my identity as a father around my ability to decode her mysteries, to find ways of connecting with her unique way of being, to serve as an advocate and interpreter between her intelligence and the world's inability to recognize it.

But seizures couldn't be decoded or interpreted. They couldn't be advocated away or understood into submission. They simply were – random electrical storms in the brain that could overtake her without warning and leave everyone who loved her feeling utterly powerless.

This was a different kind of death – not the gradual letting go of expectations about typical development, but the sudden recognition that even our adjusted expectations might be irrelevant in the face of neurological realities that operated outside any framework of meaning or purpose.

The hardest part wasn't the medical management or even the fear of future seizures. It was the way these events seemed to render meaningless all the insights I thought I had gained about her inner life and capabilities. What was the point of recognizing her intelligence if seizures could disrupt her consciousness entirely? What did her emotional wisdom matter if electrical storms could override her brain's normal functioning?

For weeks after the first seizure, I found myself questioning everything I thought I had learned about finding meaning in her condition, purpose in our relationship, wisdom in her way of being. The seizures seemed to mock the entire project of creating significance from struggle, understanding from mystery.

But slowly, very slowly, a different kind of acceptance began to emerge. Not the acceptance that comes from understanding, but the acceptance that comes from recognizing the limits of understanding itself. Some aspects of existence – consciousness, brain function, the electrical patterns that generate thought and sensation – might simply be beyond the reach of human comprehension.

The seizures taught me that love doesn't depend on understanding, that caring for someone doesn't require being able to explain their condition, that some forms of helplessness are so complete that they become a kind of spiritual practice.

Enya herself seemed to handle the seizures with the same equanimity she brought to everything else. When she recovered consciousness after each episode, there was no apparent memory of what had happened, no distress about the medical interventions, no anxiety about future occurrences.

She remained who she was – present, aware, engaged with her immediate environment – regardless of what her brain's electrical patterns might do from time to time. The seizures affected her neurology but seemed to leave her essential being untouched.

What I learned from this period was that some experiences don't lead to growth or insight or deeper understanding. Some things simply deepen the mystery of existence without offering any compensating wisdom or meaning. The seizures taught me about the density of helplessness – how some forms of powerlessness are so complete they become a different way of encountering reality itself.

By the time her condition stabilized with medication, I had been forced to accept a level of uncertainty about her wellbeing that went far beyond anything I had experienced during the autism journey. Seizures could happen at any time, for reasons that no one could predict or prevent.

This wasn't a problem to be solved or a challenge to be met with better strategies. It was simply a condition of our existence that required a different quality of surrender than anything I had learned before.

The seizures marked the end of my attempts to find ultimate meaning or purpose in her condition. They taught me that some mysteries are meant to remain mysterious, that some forms of helplessness are so total they become a form of spiritual teaching in themselves.

And perhaps most importantly, they showed me that love – real love – doesn't depend on understanding, controlling, or even helping. Sometimes love simply means being present to what is, even when what is includes realities that exceed our capacity to comprehend or change.

The dense helplessness wasn't a failure of love or understanding. It was love and understanding encountering their absolute limits – and discovering that even beyond those limits, caring continues, presence remains possible, and life finds ways to persist that have nothing to do with our ability to explain or manage its fundamental mysteries.

Eighteen Years with Enya

How Many Deaths Can One Die!

Always loved what I saw,
Thought 'twas eternity!
But then, the grandpa died,
And, so did my granny!

A Hindu, I was born,
'Hinduism', my father taught me…
The Gods and Goddesses then,
Were born inside of me!

Growing up, the use of logic,
Learning science & technology…

And lo, the faith was weakened…
Shiva or Parvati!

My favorite toy doll's lifeless,
That understanding killed me!
Every day I was more educated,
Was more dead consistently…

Amar B. Singh

The charm of childhood wore off,
Knowledge & its intensity
The kid's paradise ransacked…
Only the future to see!

The young boy I was now,
The kid was dead already!
Filled the void with school,
And my mates there, quickly!

Life was fun, friends in school & a family
Th sister, the brother, mother & father, felt heavenly!
Love & affection, learning things, doing my study
The drama of life, has in equal measures,
Comedy & tragedy!

The boy, a young man now
Going out for higher studies
Was again killed, just like earlier, albeit softly…

The need to belong, to earn & succeed, to fit in society
Took me away to unknown lands, leaving family
I wept on the train, as did my mom, both acting bravely
Neither questioned, further strengthening,

Eighteen Years with Enya

The structure of society…

Twice dead thus, and I wasn't twenty
Lost the platform I built beneath, twice already!

Deeply saddened, looking however, for a new me
My mind refused, couldn't make sense, of this catastrophe
I'd had enough – gave in to urges – mind and body

Sang and danced, used substance, life seemed an irony
Only pleasure is true, is to be sought, joy is phony!
Used fuel to quench fire, didn't wait to see
The monster born within, while I looked for me

The young man no more, a dulled ingenuity
I 'settled' in life unconscious, troubled & crazy!

The dark ages awaited, life's blind alleys
Hurtled through many hurdles, all unconsciously!
Pain became unbearable, life's inexplicable tragedy
My Creator beckoned me back, showed me mercy!

"How many deaths can you die?" He asked seemingly,
"Are you blind to see thy thoughts, as the life of thee?"
Thoughts are born; thoughts see death! Life doesn't die!

Extend your arms, touch and feel, but can't cross the sky!

My granny's dead, so is my toy, my mind & body,
Have taken myself as my thoughts, have been temporary!

For I'm unchangeable,
In the cage of my body, changing eternally!
I'm my 'being', not my form, no sophistry!

Millions of deaths one dies, only one registered!
That's not life, that life is absurd!
The book's last chapter, the movie's last scene
The birth and death are of the living,
Not of the life within!

8. The All- Knowing Glance

Enya entered adolescence like someone walking into a masquerade ball without a costume. While her peers began the elaborate process of trying on different personas, experimenting with identities, and learning the complex social choreography of teenage interaction, she remained exactly who she had always been – completely present, utterly authentic, and mysteriously uninterested in the performance aspects of human development.

She moved through her days with the same direct engagement with immediate experience that had characterized her entire childhood. She wasn't trying to be anything other than exactly what she was in each moment.

While others her age would practice conversation skills, work on reading social cues, learn strategies for fitting in with peer groups, for Enya it was clear that the entire premise felt irrelevant to her. She wasn't trying to fit in or stand out. She wasn't working to be accepted or to rebel against expectations. She was simply being herself with a consistency that made the whole enterprise of adolescent identity development seem artificial by comparison.

This authenticity extended to her emotional responses as well. While other teenagers were learning to modulate their expressions according to social context – to hide enthusiasm that might seem uncool, to suppress sensitivity that might appear weak, to perform confidence they didn't feel – Enya continued to express exactly what she was experiencing without editorial filtering.

At home, I found myself marveling at this quality during our evening conversations.

"Other teens are experimenting with identity," I mentioned to my wife as we watched Enya arrange her evening routine with characteristic precision.

"And Enya?" my wife replied.

"She's been herself all along."

"Maybe that's the real rebellion," my wife suggested.

If something delighted her, her whole body would show it. If she was overwhelmed, she would seek the sensory regulation she needed without shame or self-consciousness. If she was content, she would simply be content, without needing to explain or justify her state of being.

Those who observed these groups would sometimes express concern about her lack of "age-appropriate social awareness." They worried that she wasn't developing the self-consciousness and social sophistication that would help her navigate teenage peer relationships.

But I was beginning to see her authenticity as a form of rebellion far more radical than anything her peers were attempting. While they were rebelling against parental authority or social expectations through conventional teenage behaviors, she was rebelling against the entire premise that who you are should be different from who you appear to be.

***

At three years old, Aaryaveer had begun asking questions that revealed his growing awareness of his sister's differences.

"Why doesn't Enya talk like me?" he asked one morning as we watched her go through her breakfast routine.

"She talks in her own way," I explained, watching her arrange her food with characteristic precision.

"But I want to hear her voice," he persisted.

"You do hear it. You just have to listen differently."

Over the following months, I watched him develop this different kind of listening. He learned to read her gestures, to recognize when she needed space, to interpret her sounds as communications rather than random vocalizations. He was becoming fluent in a language the rest of us were still learning.

Enya, in the meanwhile, seemed to exist in a realm beyond such categorizations. She wasn't trying to be normal or abnormal, typical or atypical, successful or unsuccessful according to external standards. She was simply being herself with a completeness that made these categories seem irrelevant.

This became particularly clear during a trip to a shopping mall. While the other children were excited about the opportunity – ordering food, navigating social spaces – Enya was absorbed in her own form of environmental research.

She kept moving to different locations and listening to how sounds changed. She discovered that the escalator created fascinating visual patterns when viewed from certain angles. She found a section of tiled floor where her footsteps produced particularly satisfying rhythmic patterns.

We were initially concerned that she wasn't engaging with the intended learning objectives of the trip. But I watched her demonstrate environmental awareness, sensory investigation skills, and sustained attention that exceeded anything being measured in the formal assessments of her social development.

She wasn't failing to develop appropriate teenage interests – she was demonstrating forms of engagement that operated outside the categories we use to measure adolescent progress.

What became increasingly clear was that her authenticity wasn't a deficit or delay – it was an achievement. While her peers were learning the complex skills of social performance, emotional management, and identity experimentation, she was maintaining direct access to immediate experience without the filters that characterize most human interaction.

Her responses revealed how much emotional energy most people spend on managing the impression they create rather than simply being present to what they're actually feeling. She wasn't trying to appear compassionate or strong or sophisticated – she was just responding directly to the reality of each situation as she encountered it.

The professionals working with her would sometimes interpret her direct responses as evidence of social naivety or emotional immaturity. They worried that her lack of strategic thinking about social situations would leave her vulnerable to manipulation or misunderstanding.

But I was learning to see her authenticity as a form of wisdom that most adults have lost access to. She had never learned to doubt the validity of her own immediate experience, to second-guess her authentic responses, or to perform emotions she didn't feel in service of social acceptability.

While other teenagers were investing enormous energy in trying to figure out who they were supposed to be, how they were supposed to feel, and what they were supposed to want, she was simply being who she was, feeling what she felt, and engaging with what genuinely interested her.

The absence of internal conflict in her approach to identity was perhaps the most remarkable aspect of her adolescence. She didn't seem to experience the typical teenage struggles with self-doubt, social anxiety, or the pressure to conform to peer expectations. Not because these pressures didn't exist in her environment, but because she had never learned to value external approval over internal authenticity.

This created some challenging moments for family and school interactions. When well-meaning adults would try to help her develop more "age-appropriate" responses to social situations, she would cooperate politely but without any internal investment in the outcomes they were working toward.

It was as if she understood that they wanted her to learn certain skills, and she was willing to participate in the learning process, but she remained fundamentally uninterested in using these skills to create false impressions or manage social relationships strategically.

During one particularly revealing moment, I found myself speaking directly to her about this quality I was recognizing.

"You don't play like other kids," I observed as she carefully arranged her stuffed animals in precise patterns. "You play like a scientist. Like an artist. Like someone who sees magic where others see ordinary."

She looked up at me with that direct gaze that always seemed to see more than it revealed, and I felt she understood exactly what I was trying to communicate.

Her adolescence taught me that authenticity and social functioning don't have to be opposed to each other. It's possible to engage with social expectations and requirements without losing touch with genuine internal experience. But this requires a level of self-acceptance that most people never develop because they learn to doubt their authentic responses before they learn to trust them.

By the end of her fourteenth year, I had stopped worrying about whether she was developing appropriate teenage social skills and started appreciating her mastery of something far rarer: the ability to remain completely herself regardless of external pressures or expectations.

Her rebellion wasn't against authority or convention – it was against the entire premise that authenticity should be sacrificed for social acceptability. She was demonstrating that it's possible to live without masks, without performance, without the exhausting effort of trying to be anything other than exactly who you are.

And in a world where most people spend their entire lives trying to recover the authentic connection to themselves that they lost during adolescence, her refusal to participate in that loss felt like the most radical form of rebellion imaginable.

She was teaching me that the real opposites aren't good and bad, normal and abnormal, successful and unsuccessful. The real opposites are authentic and performed, genuine and strategic, present and absent.

And she had chosen authenticity with a consistency that made every other choice seem like a form of compromise with lesser possibilities.

***

The Story of Jad Bharat

The Story that shook me into looking at things we label because we don't understand and how we could enlarge our perspective

---

In ancient India, there lived a man known as Jad Bharat – "Bharat the Silent." To all who encountered him, he appeared mentally disabled. He moved slowly, spoke little, and seemed unable to understand simple instructions. People considered him dim-witted and used him for menial labor, believing he lacked the intelligence for anything more demanding.

Jad Bharat never protested this treatment. He carried heavy loads, performed difficult tasks, and endured mockery with complete equanimity. Those around him saw only limitation—a man trapped by mental deficiency, unable to participate fully in society's expectations.

One day, King Rahugana needed bearers for his palanquin and his servants recruited Jad Bharat for the task. As they traveled, the king became irritated by the uneven pace. The other bearers moved quickly, but Jad Bharat walked slowly, carefully stepping around insects and small creatures to avoid harming them.

"Move faster, you fool!" the king shouted from his palanquin. "Your slowness is disrupting our journey!"

For the first time, Jad Bharat spoke. His words revealed such profound wisdom about the nature of reality, consciousness, and the illusion of separation that King Rahugana immediately recognized he was in the presence of an enlightened being.

What appeared to be mental limitation was actually the highest form of spiritual realization. Jad Bharat's seeming inability to function according to social expectations masked a consciousness so refined that he experienced the divine in every creature, saw beyond the illusions that trap ordinary awareness, and remained in constant communion with ultimate reality.

His silence hadn't been emptiness – it had been fullness beyond the need for words. His slow movements weren't confusion – they were the careful actions of someone who understood the sacred nature of all life. His apparent disconnection from social reality reflected connection to a deeper reality that most people never glimpse.

The Deeper Story

In his previous birth, Bharata Maharaja had been a great king who renounced his throne to pursue spiritual realization. He spent years in deep meditation and austere practice, coming very close to achieving moksha – complete liberation from the cycle of birth and death.

But in his final moments, a small deer arrived at his hermitage, wounded and orphaned. Bharata cared for it with such tender attention that when death approached, his consciousness became attached to the deer's welfare. "What will happen to this helpless creature?" was his last thought.

Due to this single moment of attachment, despite a lifetime of spiritual practice, he was reborn – first as a deer, then as Jad Bharat. But he retained full memory of his previous spiritual attainment and the mistake that had cost him liberation.

In this new birth, Jad Bharat made a conscious decision: he would appear mentally disabled to avoid all social engagement that might create new attachments. He deliberately acted in ways that made people dismiss him as simple-minded, ensuring he could focus purely on inner realization without the distractions of praise, relationships, or worldly responsibilities.

To observers, he seemed unable to understand instructions or function normally. People used him for menial labor, believing he lacked intelligence. Jad Bharat never protested – this treatment served his spiritual purpose perfectly.

When King Rahugana recruited him as a palanquin bearer and became angry at his slow pace, Jad Bharat spoke for the first time. His words revealed such profound wisdom about consciousness and reality that the king immediately recognized he was in the presence of an enlightened being.

What appeared to be mental disability was actually the highest spiritual strategy – a conscious choice to remain invisible to the world's expectations while achieving the liberation that had eluded him in his previous birth.

The king fell at Jad Bharat's feet, recognizing that the person he had dismissed as disabled was actually his teacher in the highest forms of human consciousness.

This story reminds us that spiritual wisdom often appears in forms our conventional eyes cannot recognize. What we interpret as limitation may sometimes be liberation. What we see as disability may sometimes be a different kind of ability altogether.

The All-Knowing Glance

There are moments when Enya looks at me with an expression that stops my thoughts completely. Her eyes hold something that defies every assessment she has ever received, every category that has been applied to her cognitive development, every assumption about what forms of intelligence look like when they operate beyond language and conventional reasoning.

These glances arrive without warning and last only seconds, but they carry a quality of awareness that feels ancient, profound, almost unsettling in its depth. It's as if she is seeing something about the nature of existence that I can sense but not grasp, understand but not explain.

The first time I fully recognized this phenomenon, I was driving her back from school. She had been staring out the window with her usual absorbed attention, watching the movement of trees in the wind. When she turned to look at me, there was something in her gaze that felt like recognition – not just of my face or my role as her father, but of something deeper, more fundamental.

For a moment, it was as if she was seeing through all the layers of identity and concern and planning that typically fill my consciousness, looking directly at whatever it is that experiences those thoughts without being defined by them.

Over coffee the next morning, I tried to share this experience with my wife.

"Sometimes when she looks at me, I feel like she sees everything," I said, struggling to find words for something that seemed to transcend language.

"Everything what?" my wife asked.

"Everything I pretend. Everything I hide. Everything I am."

My wife paused in her morning routine. "And that scares you?"

"It humbles me," I realized.

What made this so striking was the contrast with the casual one-sided conversation that had just concluded. I had delivered a monologue as I drove, talking about the weather and work and weekend plans – the kind of routine chatter that fills the space between destinations.

But the intelligence I encountered in her gaze operated according to completely different principles. It wasn't reasoning its way to conclusions or processing information through logical sequences. It was directly apprehending something immediate, present, and more fundamental than anything that could be captured through conventional assessment.

These moments began happening more frequently as she moved through her fifteenth year. Sometimes during our evening walks, she would pause and look at me with that same quality of profound recognition. Sometimes during quiet moments at home, she would catch my eye with an expression that suggested she was seeing something about our relationship, about consciousness itself, that I could feel but not articulate.

What disturbed me initially was how these all-knowing glances seemed to reveal that she possessed forms of awareness that I was only beginning to glimpse during moments of deep meditation or unusual stillness. While I had to work to quiet my mental activity enough to access present-moment awareness, she seemed to inhabit that space naturally.

The most profound instance occurred during a particularly difficult period when my wife was struggling with work stress and family concerns. She was sitting at the dining table, caught up in worry about the endless logistical challenges of managing life with a disabled family member.

Enya appeared beside her chair, as she often did when she sensed emotional disturbance. But instead of her usual gentle touch, she simply stood there and waited until her mother looked up. When their eyes met, I encountered something that felt like compassion, but not the kind that emerges from understanding someone's specific circumstances.

It was as if she was seeing the essential nature of human suffering – not her mom's particular worries about money or the future, but the fundamental pattern of how consciousness creates anxiety by projecting itself into imagined scenarios that exist only in thought.

Her gaze seemed to hold both complete understanding of what her mom was experiencing and complete freedom from being disturbed by it. She wasn't trying to fix her mom's concerns or offer comfort in any conventional sense. She was simply present to what was actually happening in that moment, including her mental activity, without being caught up in the content of her mom's thoughts.

What made these encounters so challenging was that they suggested forms of consciousness that operated independently of the cognitive development that professionals used to evaluate her capabilities. According to every formal assessment, her abstract thinking was severely limited. But her presence during these moments revealed abstract understanding that seemed to transcend anything I had encountered in people with advanced degrees and sophisticated analytical skills.

She appeared to have direct access to states of awareness that most adults spend years trying to achieve through meditation, therapy, or spiritual practice. Not because she had worked to develop these capacities, but because she had never learned to obscure them with the mental activity that characterizes most human consciousness.

During family gatherings, I would sometimes observe her watching the social dynamics with an expression that suggested she was seeing patterns that the participants themselves weren't aware of. While others were caught up in the content of conversations, conflicts, or shared activities, she seemed to be observing the underlying emotional currents with remarkable clarity.

When I spoke directly to her about what I was observing, the responses were subtle but unmistakable.

"Sometimes I think you understand everything," I said during one of our quiet moments together.

She looked directly into my eyes for a long moment – not the quick glance of social acknowledgment, but the sustained gaze of someone measuring whether to reveal something significant.

"You do, don't you? You just don't need to prove it," I continued.

Her understanding of her brother Aaryaveer provided perhaps the clearest example of this phenomenon. While he was developing conventional intelligence – learning to read, mastering mathematical concepts, acquiring the social skills that would serve him well in academic and professional environments – her awareness of his emotional states and needs often exceeded my own.

She would sense when he was frustrated with homework before he expressed it verbally. She would offer comfort when he was dealing with social challenges at school before he had told anyone what was happening. She seemed to perceive his internal experiences directly, without needing the verbal communication that the rest of us required to understand what he was going through.

What struck me most was the contrast between her insight into his emotional reality and his developing analytical capabilities. He could explain complex concepts, demonstrate sophisticated reasoning, and articulate his thoughts and feelings with increasing sophistication. But he didn't seem to have access to the direct perception of others' internal states that characterized her awareness.

This suggested that there might be forms of intelligence that develop independently of – or even inversely to – the cognitive capabilities that our educational systems are designed to measure and enhance. That consciousness itself might include capacities that emerge when the usual filters of mental analysis are bypassed rather than strengthened.

***

A Brother's Growing Awareness

When Aaryaveer turned four, I watched him discover something that had taken me years to recognize. He was playing with his building blocks one afternoon when I came home from a particularly difficult day at work. I thought I was hiding my frustration well, but within minutes of my arrival, Enya had positioned herself near my chair, offering her silent presence.

"Why does she do that?" Aaryaveer asked, looking up from his blocks.

"Do what?" I replied, though I knew exactly what he meant.

"She always comes over when you're sad, even before you look sad." A four-year-old had articulated something that developmental psychologists struggled to explain.

"You're right," I told him. "She does do that. What do you think it means?"

He considered this seriously. "I think she can feel what we feel. Like when you are talking about her, she's already looking at you even with her head pointed down."

The Question That Cut Through

Aaryaveer was four when he asked the question that revealed how much deeper her awareness ran than any of us had realized. It was a Tuesday afternoon, and Enya had been on her iPad exploring song videos for the better part of an hour. The precision of her system was remarkable – each song positioned exactly in an order that made sense only to her.

Aaryaveer watched from the doorway for several minutes, then approached and pulled the iPad away with the casual destructiveness that four-year-olds bring to anything that looks orderly. Enya immediately began to swipe to reach YouTube, her movements careful and patient, showing no irritation at the disruption.

"Why doesn't she get mad?" he asked me, his voice carrying genuine confusion.

"She understands that you're still learning," I explained, the kind of diplomatic response parents develop for difficult questions.

He pulled it away and pressed the iPad button again, more deliberately this time, watching her face for a reaction. Again, Enya simply began to look for the icon, her expression serene, even a hint of a smile.

"Is she dumb?" The question emerged with the brutal honesty that children wield before they learn about sensitivity.

For a moment, her usual composure wavered. Not dramatically – she didn't cry or react in ways that would have been obvious to casual observers. But I saw the brief shadow that crossed her features, the way her shoulders drew slightly upward, the pause before she returned to her iPad. She had felt the weight of being measured and found wanting, even if she couldn't articulate that feeling.

"She's not dumb," I told Aaryaveer, my voice sharper than I intended. "She's different. Her brain works in ways that are special."

But the moment had revealed something profound. Her all-knowing glances weren't just about perceiving others' emotions – they included sophisticated understanding of how language carries judgment, how questions can wound even when they're asked without malice, how being categorized affects the one being categorized.

She's My Sister

The incident that became Aaryaveer's awakening happened when he was five. A group of children had begun mimicking Enya's hand movements, their laughter carrying that particular cruelty that children wield unconsciously.

Before I could intervene, Aaryaveer planted himself between them and his sister.

"She's not funny," he announced with the moral clarity that only children possess. "She's doing her thing, and you're being mean."

The other children, surprised by this small defender's fierce confidence, actually stopped their mimicry.

Walking to the car later, I asked him why he had stepped in.

"Because she's my sister," he said, as if this explained everything. And perhaps it did.

Over the following weeks, I noticed subtle changes in how she related to her brother. When he ran too close to the stairs, she would position herself between him and potential danger – not dramatically, but with quiet purpose. When he climbed on furniture, she would appear nearby, not interfering with his exploration but ready to break a fall.

Most remarkably, she began to anticipate his needs in ways that went beyond her previous intuitive responses. If he seemed tired during play, she would give up the TV remote before he asked for it. If he sat close to her, she would let him – which was significant for someone who typically needed precise control over her personal space.

This wasn't learned behavior from observing adult caregiving. This was emotional intelligence responding to the recognition that someone she loved was vulnerable – perhaps more vulnerable than she was, despite his verbal abilities and social ease. The question "Is she dumb?" had awakened something protective in her, an understanding that in some essential ways, she was the older sister with deeper wisdom about navigating the world's complexities.

Phone conversations with friends often ended up touching on this quality of awareness that seemed to operate beyond conventional measures.

"You always say she doesn't talk much," a friend observed during one call.

"She doesn't need to. Her eyes say everything," I replied.

"Like what?"

"Like she understands things I'm still trying to figure out."

The all-knowing glance wasn't something she did – it was something she is. These moments revealed that her usual engagement with sensory details, her absorption in immediate experience, her apparent disconnection from social complexity might actually be expressions of a profound connection to present-moment awareness that most people lose during the process of conventional development.

The professionals who evaluated her cognitive capabilities were measuring her ability to manipulate symbols, process information sequentially, and demonstrate understanding through language-based responses. But they were completely missing forms of consciousness that operated through direct perception, immediate knowing, and awareness that transcended the subject-object divisions that characterize most human thinking.

During a quiet evening reflection, I found myself speaking to this quality directly.

"What are you thinking when you look at me like that?" I asked during one of those profound moments of eye contact.

The silence that followed wasn't empty – it was full of communication that didn't require words to be complete.

"You don't need to think it, do you? You just know it."

Her glances were teaching me that intelligence might include capacities that have nothing to do with problem-solving, reasoning, or information processing. That consciousness itself might be far more mysterious and sophisticated than anything our models of cognitive development can account for.

By the end of her fifteenth year, I had stopped trying to understand what she was seeing during these moments of profound recognition and started learning to receive whatever teaching was being offered. Her awareness was pointing toward dimensions of consciousness that I could sense but not grasp, understand experientially but not explain conceptually.

The all-knowing glance is her gift to anyone willing to receive it – a window into forms of consciousness that exist beyond the categories we use to measure intelligence, beyond the frameworks we use to understand human development, beyond the assumptions we make about what wisdom looks like when it appears in unexpected forms.

She was demonstrating that some of the most profound human capacities might emerge not through development and learning, but through remaining connected to the awareness that exists before thoughts, beneath concepts, beyond the need to understand in order to know.

Her eyes held the secret that consciousness itself might be far vaster and more mysterious than anything our assessments could measure – and that sometimes the deepest intelligence appears in forms that our categories of normal development are designed to overlook entirely.

***

9. Love Without Language: Her Universe, Her Rules

By her sixteenth year, Enya had developed what in the clinical reports is diplomatically termed "restricted interests of unusual intensity." But what the professionals saw as limitations, I was learning to recognize as a form of devotion that most people never achieve in any area of their lives.

Her relationship with water had evolved into something approaching reverence. Not just the casual enjoyment that most people have for swimming or bathing, but a sophisticated exploration of water's properties that seemed to border on scientific research combined with spiritual practice.

She could spend hours at the bathroom sink, not just playing with the faucet, but conducting what appeared to be systematic investigations into how water behaves under different conditions. She would adjust the pressure to create specific flow patterns, hold her hands at various angles to observe how the stream divided and reformed, experiment with temperature changes and their effects on the water's movement.

One afternoon, my father observed this behavior with concern.

"She's been watching the same video sequence for three hours daily," he noted.

"You call it obsession. I call it devotion," I replied.

"What's the difference?"

"Love. When you love something, repetition becomes ritual."

My father smiled, "Yes, I see that with Enya."

To observers unfamiliar with the depth of her engagement, this might have looked like simple repetitive behavior or perseveration. But I had learned to see the sophisticated attention she was bringing to these explorations. She wasn't mindlessly repeating the same actions – she was systematically varying conditions to observe different outcomes.

At home, my wife noticed the same patterns extending to her room organization.

"She's reorganized her room again," my wife mentioned one evening as we prepared dinner.

"Same pattern as always – removing what she doesn't like to drawers," I observed.

"Should we encourage her to try something different?"

I paused from my work, considering this. "Why? She's created her own perfect universe."

The professionals working with her were concerned about the amount of time she spent on these "non-functional" activities. They worried that her narrow focus was preventing her from developing broader interests and more diverse skills. Their intervention strategies were designed to redirect her attention toward activities that would support conventional learning objectives.

But I was beginning to suspect that her intense focus might actually be demonstrating a form of intelligence that our educational systems are completely unable to recognize, much less support.

Her absorption in specific sensory experiences revealed a capacity for sustained attention that exceeded anything I had seen in typical learners. While most students struggle to maintain focus on academic tasks for more than a few minutes at a time, she could engage with her chosen investigations for hours without any apparent fatigue or loss of interest.

During a family gathering, my sister observed Enya's focused attention to her iPad music videos with mild concern.

"She seems so focused on her own things," my sister remarked.

"She knows what brings her joy," I replied.

"But shouldn't she be more... social?"

"She is social. With the things that matter to her."

What struck me was how her supposed limitations might actually be advantages in disguise. While others were developing broad, shallow knowledge across multiple domains, she was developing profound, intimate understanding of the specific phenomena that captured her attention.

Her fascination with certain textures had evolved into what could only be described as textile research. She had developed an extraordinary sensitivity to different fabrics, able to identify materials through touch alone, recognizing subtle variations in weave patterns, fiber content, and manufacturing processes.

When we went shopping for clothes, she would move through stores like a quality control specialist, immediately identifying which fabrics would feel comfortable against her skin and which would create sensory distress. Her assessments were more accurate than anything the sales staff could provide, based on direct tactile investigation rather than reading labels or relying on brand reputations.

The educational team saw this as evidence that she was "overly dependent on sensory input" and needed to develop more "functional" ways of evaluating clothing options. But I was learning that her approach might actually be more sophisticated than the conventional methods that rely on visual appearance and social signaling rather than direct assessment of material quality.

Her interest in specific visual patterns had similarly deepened into what resembled advanced studies in optics and design. She had discovered that certain combinations of light and shadow created effects that seemed to fascinate her at a level that suggested aesthetic appreciation combined with scientific curiosity.

She would position herself in locations where natural light created particularly interesting patterns – near windows during specific times of day, in spaces where architectural features created complex shadows, in environments where moving elements like trees or water generated dynamic visual effects.

When I tried to understand what she was seeing in these patterns, I began to notice visual phenomena that I had been walking past for years without really observing. Her attention was calling my awareness to subtleties of light, color, and geometric relationship that existed everywhere but were typically overwhelmed by the mental noise of planning, analyzing, and goal-directed thinking.

In my own internal reflection, I found myself thinking: "What we call limited interests, she experiences as unlimited depth."

Her devotion to these interests wasn't interfering with her ability to function in the world – it was revealing aspects of the world that functional thinking typically overlooks. While others were focused on using environments for practical purposes, she was discovering beauty and complexity that existed independent of utility.

What the professionals called "restricted interests" were actually areas where she had developed expertise that exceeded most adult capabilities. Her knowledge of water dynamics, textile properties, and visual pattern recognition was both more detailed and more directly experienced than anything that could be acquired through conventional education.

The contrast with typical teenage interests was particularly instructive. While her peers were developing fascinations with social media, popular culture, and peer relationships, she was pursuing investigations that seemed almost monastic in their single-pointed focus and depth.

But her approach to learning wasn't characterized by the anxiety and social pressure that accompanied most adolescent interests. She wasn't trying to impress anyone, compete with others, or achieve recognition for her knowledge. She was simply following her natural curiosity into territories that provided satisfaction and understanding for their own sake.

This quality of surrender to her authentic interests created a different relationship to learning than anything I had observed in conventional educational settings. She wasn't struggling against her natural inclinations in order to meet external expectations. She was following her intrinsic motivation wherever it led, developing expertise through pure engagement rather than forced effort.

The breakthrough came when I stopped trying to broaden her interests and started learning from the depth of engagement she was demonstrating. Instead of seeing her focused attention as limitation, I began to recognize it as a form of mastery that most people never achieve in any domain.

Her universe operated according to different rules than the ones that governed conventional learning and development. Where others were encouraged to develop diverse capabilities across multiple domains, she was demonstrating that profound understanding might emerge through sustained devotion to specific phenomena.

What others called obsession, I was learning to recognize as devotion. What others saw as restricted interest, I was beginning to understand as focused investigation. What others worried about as limitation, I was starting to appreciate as a form of spiritual practice disguised as sensory exploration.

Her capacity for sustained attention, her ability to find endless fascination in seemingly simple phenomena, her willingness to engage deeply rather than broadly – these weren't developmental delays or symptomatic behaviors. They were demonstrations of forms of intelligence that our culture has almost completely lost.

In a world characterized by scattered attention, superficial engagement, and the restless pursuit of novelty, she was demonstrating the power of sustained devotion, deep investigation, and the willingness to find infinite complexity within apparently simple phenomena.

By the end of her sixteenth year, I had stopped seeing her focused interests as problems to be solved and started seeing them as teachings about the difference between scattered engagement and devoted attention, between broad superficial knowledge and deep intimate understanding, between learning driven by external expectations and investigation motivated by authentic curiosity.

By the time Enya was sixteen, my father had become one of her most sophisticated interpreters within our family.

"She doesn't greet people the way you expect," he would explain to visiting relatives. "But watch how she positions herself in the room. If she chooses to sit near you, that's her welcome."

Gone were the suggestions for additional remedies or alternative treatments. Instead, he had developed what could only be called reverence for her way of being.

"You know what I learned from all those years of trying to change her?" he asked during her sixteenth birthday celebration.

"What's that?"

"That some souls come already perfected. They're not here to learn – they're here to teach."

She was showing us that there might be forms of intelligence that emerge through sustained devotion to specific phenomena rather than broad exposure to diverse information. That expertise might develop through love and fascination rather than effort and discipline. That some of the most profound forms of understanding might be accessible only to those willing to follow their authentic interests wherever they lead, regardless of whether others can understand the value of what they're discovering.

Her universe, her rules. And in that universe, devotion was intelligence, obsession was love, and limitation was actually a form of liberation from the anxiety of trying to be everything to everyone instead of being completely present to whatever genuinely captures your attention.

***

Love Without Language

At seventeen, Enya had developed a vocabulary of love that required no words, operated through no conventional expressions of affection, and communicated more directly than anything I had ever experienced through language. Her way of loving challenged every assumption I held about how emotional connection happens between human beings.

Her expressions of care were so subtle they could easily be missed by anyone not paying careful attention. She didn't say "I love you" or give hugs on demand or perform the social rituals that most people use to demonstrate affection. Instead, she had created an entire language of presence that spoke more eloquently than any words could convey.

One evening, as my wife and I sat in the living room, she made an observation that crystallized something I had been noticing.

"She hasn't told me 'I love you' in years," my wife remarked, watching Enya doing her assigned activity.

"Look how she sits next to you every morning," I replied, noticing how Enya consistently chose to position herself near my wife during their quiet morning routines.

"But the words..." my wife began.

"Love isn't words. Love is presence," I said, finally understanding something that had been developing slowly over the years.

The first time I fully recognized this language was during a period when I was dealing with some difficult work challenges. I had been carrying stress and frustration that I thought I was concealing successfully, maintaining my usual external composure while internally wrestling with problems that felt overwhelming.

Enya began appearing at my side during these difficult moments, not with obvious gestures of comfort, but with a quality of presence that seemed designed to provide exactly what I needed. She would position herself nearby while I worked, creating a field of calm attention that somehow made the problems feel more manageable.

What struck me was how her expressions of love seemed to bypass the usual channels of emotional communication entirely. She wasn't trying to understand my specific concerns or offer solutions to my problems. She was simply offering her presence as a form of support that operated independently of comprehension or verbal exchange.

When my mother visited for an extended stay, I watched Enya develop a completely different set of caring behaviors tailored to her grandmother's particular needs. She seemed to sense that my mother required more physical proximity and gentle touch than I did, and she adjusted her expressions of affection accordingly.

She would sit closer to my mother during meals, sometimes resting her hand lightly on her arm. She would bring her specific objects – a favorite cushion, a particular book – without being asked, as if she could perceive what would bring comfort in each moment.

What amazed me was how these gestures never felt calculated or performed. They emerged naturally from her awareness of what each person needed, demonstrating a form of emotional intelligence that seemed to operate through direct perception rather than learned social skills.

Her relationship with her younger brother provided perhaps the clearest window into her capacity for wordless love. From the moment he was born, she had immediately recognized him as someone who required different forms of attention and care than the adults in her environment.

She had never shown jealousy or competition for parental attention. Instead, she seemed to understand intuitively that his arrival meant the family dynamic had shifted, and she adjusted her own behavior to support his needs rather than compete with them.

I would watch her observe him with intense focus when he was upset or struggling with something, as if she was gathering information about what would help him feel better. Then she would offer her own form of assistance – not the verbal comfort or practical help that adults might provide, but something more fundamental.

Sometimes she would simply position herself where he could see her, offering her calm presence as an anchor during his emotional storms. Sometimes she would bring him objects that seemed to provide sensory comfort. Sometimes she would just sit nearby, creating a field of patient attention that seemed to help him regulate his own emotional states.

The Protector Emerges

By age seven, Aaryaveer had become our family's unofficial Enya translator. When relatives visited and expressed concern about her lack of response to their greetings, he would provide patient explanation.

"She heard you," he would tell confused aunties and uncles. "She just doesn't do the hi-bye thing. But watch – if you sit next to her while she's doing her iPad, she'll let you stay. That means she likes you."

His translations were remarkably accurate. He had developed an intuitive understanding of her communication style that surpassed many of the professionals working with her.

"How do you know what she wants?" a relative asked him during a get-together.

"I just watch," he replied with the simplicity of a seven-year-old. "She shows you everything. You just have to pay attention."

By the time Aaryaveer turned eight, he had become her most articulate advocate, but what moved me most was watching their wordless communication develop into something approaching telepathy.

During a family gathering, I observed them navigate a crowded room with the kind of coordination that comes from deep mutual understanding. Without any verbal communication, Enya would sense when the environment was becoming too stimulating for her brother's energy level, and she would quietly guide him toward calmer spaces. He, in turn, seemed to understand when she needed protection from well-meaning relatives who might overwhelm her with too much direct attention.

Their sibling relationship had evolved into something that transcended conventional family dynamics. They had become mutual protectors, each attuned to the other's needs in ways that required no explanation or negotiation.

One afternoon, I found myself speaking to both of them during a quiet moment.

"Other kids say the words," I said to Enya, knowing she was listening even as she focused on her afternoon music routine.

She looked up from her iPad, offering that direct gaze that always seemed to convey more than speech could.

"But you share the feeling itself, don't you?" I continued.

Aaryaveer, now old enough to articulate what he had always intuited, added his own observation: "She doesn't need to say it. You can just feel it when she loves you."

This wasn't learned behavior in any conventional sense. No one had taught her to detect emotional distress in others, much less how to respond with such precision and care. It appeared to be an innate capacity that had developed outside the normal channels of social learning.

Her emotional interventions never felt intrusive or inappropriate. She seemed to have an intuitive understanding of when to offer physical comfort, when to simply be present, and when to maintain distance. This discriminating awareness suggested a level of social intelligence that existed independently of her ability to engage in conventional social interactions.

***

Consciousness-Level Love

During a phone conversation with a friend who had asked about our family dynamics, I found myself trying to explain something that seemed almost impossible to communicate.

"How do you handle not hearing 'I love you'?" my friend asked.

"We do hear it," I replied. "Just not in words."

"What do you mean?"

"When she puts your glasses on your eyes, that's her way of saying it. When she sits quietly beside you when you're sad, that's her way of living it."

Her love doesn't come wrapped in expectations or conditions. She doesn't love me because I'm successful, because I meet her needs, or because I'm a good father. She loves the being-ness that exists before all those identities and achievements.

This is what consciousness operating at its most natural level looks like – love that flows like sunlight, freely given, without calculation or expectation of return. Most of us learned love as exchange: "I love you because..." or "I love you when..." But Enya embodies what mystics call unconditional positive regard – love as the natural state of awareness, not as an emotion triggered by circumstances.

She loves my being, not my doing. My essence, not my achievements. My presence, not my performance.

What I gradually realized was that Enya's expressions of love were actually more sophisticated than most verbal demonstrations of affection. While words can lie, manipulate, or be offered out of obligation, her nonverbal care emerged only from genuine concern and seemed perfectly calibrated to what each person actually needed.

She had learned to read the emotional climate of our household with remarkable accuracy, adjusting her own energy and behavior according to what would support the overall harmony. During tense moments between my wife and me, she would often appear and simply be present in a way that seemed to remind us of what was actually important.

Not through intervention or mediation, but through the quality of attention she brought to whatever was happening. Her presence seemed to call everyone back to the immediate reality of the moment rather than the mental stories that were creating conflict.

Her expressions of gratitude operated according to similar principles. She couldn't say "thank you" in conventional ways, but she had developed rituals of appreciation that felt more meaningful than any verbal acknowledgment I had ever received.

When someone did something that pleased her, she would often return to them later with a small offering – a particularly interesting object she had found, a gentle touch, or simply the gift of her focused attention. These gestures carried a quality of recognition that suggested she understood not just what had been done for her, but the intention behind it.

What made her love so powerful was its complete lack of agenda or expectation. She didn't love in order to receive love in return, or to maintain relationships, or to fulfill social obligations. Her caring seemed to emerge from some deeper source that operated independently of reciprocity or social exchange.

This became particularly clear during times when I was less available to her due to work demands or personal stress. Instead of becoming demanding or attention-seeking, she would simply adjust her own behavior to require less from me while continuing to offer her presence when I needed it.

Her love seemed to include an intuitive understanding of the natural rhythms of availability and attention in relationships. She could sense when someone needed space and when they needed connection, offering each with the same graceful sensitivity to timing and appropriateness.

During a family conversation, I tried to articulate what I was learning from her approach to love.

"I used to worry that she couldn't express love," my wife admitted.

"And now?" I asked.

"Now I think she expresses nothing but love."

By her seventeenth year, I had begun to recognize that her wordless expressions of love were actually teaching me about forms of emotional connection that transcend language entirely. While most human relationships depend heavily on verbal communication to navigate emotional complexity, she was demonstrating that some of the most profound forms of caring happen in the spaces between words.

Her love wasn't dependent on understanding or being understood. It didn't require explanation or interpretation. It simply was – a constant quality of benevolent attention that she offered to the people in her environment regardless of whether they could recognize or reciprocate it.

What I was learning was that love might be far simpler and more direct than the complex emotional negotiations that characterize most human relationships. That caring might emerge naturally when attention is freed from the mental activity that typically obscures our immediate connection to others.

Her expressions of affection weren't limited by the categories that usually define emotional relationships. She didn't love differently because someone was family versus friend, adult versus child, familiar versus stranger. Her care seemed to extend naturally to whoever was present, adjusted to their particular needs but not constrained by social definitions of appropriate emotional boundaries.

This quality of universal compassion wasn't something she had learned through spiritual practice or philosophical study. It seemed to be her natural state, the way caring expressed itself when it wasn't filtered through the mental constructs that typically complicate human emotional connection.

Her love was teaching me that emotional connection might be far more immediate and less complicated than the psychological frameworks that dominate our understanding of relationships. That caring might operate through direct perception rather than interpretation, through presence rather than expression, through being rather than doing.

By the end of her seventeenth year, I had stopped trying to elicit verbal expressions of affection from her and started learning to receive the profound forms of love she was already offering. Her wordless care was more reliable, more sensitive, and more nourishing than most of the verbal demonstrations of affection I had experienced in other relationships.

She was teaching me that love isn't something that needs to be expressed, declared, or performed. Love is something that is lived, embodied, and offered through the quality of attention we bring to others' actual experience in each moment.

Her silence wasn't an absence of communication—it was communication distilled to its essence, freed from the complexity and misunderstanding that often accompany verbal expression. In her wordless love, I was discovering forms of emotional connection that transcended anything that language could convey.

***

10. The Wave Realizes the Ocean

> Eighteen years to understand
> she had never forgotten
> what I spent
> decades trying to remember.

As Enya approaches her eighteenth birthday, I have begun to understand that everything I had spent years trying to teach her, she had been demonstrating all along. The journey from my attempts to fix her to learning from her had revealed different levels of consciousness operating within human response to uncontrollable circumstances.

For most of her childhood, I had been operating from what I came to understand as Level 1 thinking – the belief that problems could be solved through strategy, effort, and the application of will. I had tried to change her, fix her, help her adapt to conventional expectations. I had pursued therapies, interventions, and educational approaches with the confidence that the right combination of effort and expertise could overcome any challenge.

When those strategies failed to produce the results I expected, I had gradually moved into Level 2 consciousness – learning to accept what couldn't be changed, developing equanimity in the face of circumstances beyond my control. I had learned to find peace with her autism, to appreciate her unique way of being, to stop fighting against her natural development.

But it wasn't until that transformative week with her, and later with her seizure experience, when I finally learned to truly see her, that I began to glimpse Level 3 consciousness – the recognition that we are all waves in the same ocean, temporary expressions of something vast and eternal that appears in countless forms but is always essentially the same.

During a quiet conversation with my wife one evening, as we watched Enya go through her evening routine with the same deliberate precision she brought to everything, I tried to articulate what I was finally understanding.

"I finally understand what she's been teaching me," I said.

"Which is?" my wife asked, settling beside me on the couch.

"That we're not separate from each other. We're not even separate from her."

My wife looked puzzled. "What do you mean?"

"She's not different from us. We're all waves in the same ocean."

What I was slowly understanding was that Enya had never been operating from the illusion of separation that characterizes most human consciousness. She had never believed that she was fundamentally different from the world around her, never struggled with the existential anxiety that comes from thinking of yourself as an isolated individual trying to survive in an indifferent universe.

Her way of being in the world reflected a natural understanding of impermanence and interconnectedness that I had spent decades trying to achieve through intellectual study and spiritual practice. She didn't cling to outcomes because she didn't experience herself as separate from the process of life itself.

When changes happened in her environment – moving to a new house, starting at a different school, adjusting to new people –

she adapted with a fluidity that suggested she understood at some fundamental level that forms are always temporary, that attachment to specific conditions creates unnecessary suffering.

While I had struggled for years with questions about why she was autistic, what her condition meant, how to help her achieve her potential, she seemed to live beyond the need for such explanations. She existed in the immediate reality of each moment without requiring it to make sense according to any larger narrative or purpose.

Sometimes, in direct moments with her, I would voice what I was learning: "You've been showing me something all along, haven't you?"

She would rest her head on my shoulder or hold my hand with her fingers clasping mine — her characteristic response that somehow conveyed both comfort and confirmation.

"That there's no separation. No us and them. Just... this."

This became particularly clear as I watched her response to the seizures that had introduced such anxiety into our family life. While I experienced each episode as a crisis requiring medical intervention, emotional processing, and vigilant monitoring for future occurrences, she seemed to move through them with the same equanimity she brought to everything else.

She didn't appear to carry forward worry about when the next seizure might happen or frustration about the limitations the medication imposed. She simply lived in whatever neurological reality was present in each moment, adapting to changes in her brain chemistry with the same fluid acceptance she showed toward all other forms of change.

What I was learning was that her apparent limitations might actually be expressions of a profound spiritual maturity that most people never achieve. Her inability to plan far into the future, her lack of ambition for conventional achievements, her disinterest in accumulating possessions or status – all of these could be seen as natural expressions of someone who understood the temporary nature of all forms.

While I had lost the spontaneous joy of childhood through the process of developing an adult identity focused on achievement and security, she had somehow retained direct access to the present-moment awareness that makes genuine contentment possible.

Her resistance to therapy goals and educational objectives wasn't stubbornness or cognitive limitation – it was wisdom. She instinctively understood that trying to become something other than what you are in each moment creates the kind of internal conflict that destroys peace and authentic engagement with life.

The irony wasn't lost on me that I had spent years trying to help her develop qualities that I myself had lost through the very process of conventional development. While I had learned to postpone satisfaction in service of future goals, to suppress authentic responses in favor of social appropriateness, to analyze experiences rather than simply having them, she had maintained direct access to the awareness that exists before such complications arise.

Level 3 consciousness – the understanding that individual identity is like a wave on the ocean, real but temporary, connected to but not separate from the vast movement of life itself – wasn't something she had achieved through spiritual practice or philosophical inquiry. It was simply how she naturally experienced reality.

She has never developed the strong sense of individual will that characterizes most adult consciousness. Her preferences are real but not rigid. Her interests are intense but not possessive. Her responses are authentic but not defensive. She lives as if she understood that the wave is always the ocean, never separate from it, never in conflict with it.

Watching her move through the world with this quality of surrender and presence has gradually taught me about forms of consciousness that exist beyond the ego-driven awareness that dominates most human experience. She was demonstrating what it looks like to live without the internal resistance that creates suffering.

In conversations with friends who asked about our journey, I found myself saying things like: "Seventeen years of trying to help her connect to our world. She has been showing me we're already connected."

Her autism wasn't a disorder or limitation – it was a different way of embodying consciousness that bypassed many of the mental constructions that complicate most people's relationship with immediate reality. What looked like developmental delay from the outside was actually a form of spiritual sophistication that preserved direct access to present-moment awareness.

Her complete presence to immediate experience, her lack of anxiety about the future, her inability to hold grudges or maintain emotional conflicts, her natural compassion that extended to everyone regardless of how they treated her – all of these weren't the result of cognitive limitation but expressions of consciousness that had never become entangled in the illusions of separation and permanence.

What I had interpreted as her inability to understand complex social dynamics was actually wisdom about the artificial nature of most human emotional drama. She responded to what people were actually feeling rather than getting caught up in the stories they told themselves about their feelings.

Her difficulty with language wasn't a communication deficit – it was freedom from the mental activity that typically obscures direct perception. Her repetitive behaviors weren't symptoms of dysfunction – they were expressions of the natural rhythm and order that emerges when consciousness isn't constantly interfering with itself.

By her eighteenth year, I have understood that what I had thought of as teaching her acceptance and resilience was actually her teaching me. She has been living all along what I was struggling to understand: that individual identity is temporary, that resistance to what is creates suffering, that peace comes from recognizing our fundamental unity with the movement of life itself.

She is the wave that had never forgotten it was ocean. While I have spent decades believing I was separate from the universe and needed to achieve something or become someone in order to be worthy of love and happiness, she had remained connected to the source from which all waves arise and to which they inevitably return.

Her eighteenth birthday isn't a milestone marking her transition to adulthood according to conventional measures of independence and achievement. It is a celebration of eighteen years of pure presence, authentic being, and the kind of spiritual mastery that appears when consciousness never becomes divorced from its source.

What I had seen as limitation was actually liberation. What I had interpreted as deficit was actually a gift. What I had tried to correct was actually teaching. She had been offering lessons in the highest form of human consciousness all along – the recognition that we are all temporary expressions of eternal awareness, waves in an infinite ocean of being, never separate from the source that gives rise to all forms and to which all forms eventually return.

The wave had finally realized it was ocean. Not through achieving anything or becoming anything, but through recognizing what had always been true. And in that recognition, everything changed while nothing changed at all. The ocean remained the ocean, and every wave was equally its expression, equally precious, equally temporary, equally perfect exactly as it was.

***

The Leaf is the Tree

It's a lovely life
Siblings, parents, kids and wife!
A well-paying job, great career,
All secured from any strife!

A restlessness however, looms
Stomach's full & yet, there's room.
Insatiable hunger, unquenchable thirst
Safe & secure, yet the dearth!

Took me time, survival was to be ensured…
Successful I am, but also bored!

My yesterday is my today,
My today, tomorrow,
The body is safe,
And, so is my sorrow…

Is it me or, the nature of my existence?

Inexplicable my sorrow and its substance…
My mind works hard, doesn't accept defeat
Can't find an answer, offers hypotheses!

Like a racing car, fast, new & shining
The fuel over, stands on the sidelines
Maybe the ephemeral wants the eternal
Permanent security, unceasing survival!

Body is not eternal but, I realize…
My mind in conflict, part of me dies!
The 5-year-old, his joy's gone
Waits for the dusk,
Smiles ruefully at the dawn…

Indefatigable, the mind and its imagination
Tick marks on a bucket list, seems the solution!

It starts, unconscious admission of defeat…
Packing the life with sensations, achieving feats!

The problem unchanged, was and remains,
My mind can't change, my existence!
Sensations, its variety, not found working
My mind sees its limits, leaves the thing…

It drops the greed
The belief in God, and its need
Yes, 'I am doomed', it realizes
It's a play alright but, I'm not the player,
I'm the pieces!

Finally, the mind lies peaceful and still
No purpose to achieve, no flag on the hill…
My body will die, so will my mind
I see them now, I've been blind!

Completely taken over, by this need for survival
Have been a slave to sorrow,
Or, to ambition and zeal…

If there's no tomorrow, I ask my mind
Is there still something, I should run behind?

The mind lies low, the body rests
Now is the only reality, it's the present!
Rid of the chains of jealousy
The sorrow, the anger, the ambitious fantasy!

The leaf has finally accepted the tree

Amar B. Singh

The illusions of will, the destiny…
The leaf is the tree, the tree the leaf
I'm God myself, no reason for belief!

The joy's back, like the 5-year-old
The run is for the fun, not for the gold!

No boredom, no sorrow, just the open sky
The yesterday's dead,
Today I'm born anew!

Epilogue: From Wave to Ocean

> You're 'the happy', you win or lose
> The thrill of you, nobody can cut loose!
> This illusion of time, of place and space,
> Watched long enough, dissolves itself...
>
> So, try and yet, don't try
> Seek and yet, don't seek
> Forego the 'I', this ego
> Don't swim hard,
> Go with the flow!
>
> -From "Joy in the Work or, in Me?"

As I finished writing these pages one month before Enya's eighteenth birthday, I understood something I couldn't have grasped when I began: this book was never meant to be a conclusion. It was meant to be preparation.

Preparation for recognizing that the apprenticeship deepens rather than ends. For understanding that turning eighteen would not mark her passage into something new, but my passage into seeing what had always been true. For the awareness that every day with her had been both ordinary and sacred, both challenging and blessed.

The Natural Transformation

Writing this memoir revealed something unexpected: my own transformation had happened so gradually, so naturally, that I had barely noticed it occurring. Somewhere in those eighteen years, I had stopped trying to fix Enya and started learning from her. Somewhere in that journey, I had lost the ambition to make her fit the world and gained the wisdom to let the world be changed by her presence.

The selfish desires for conventional success, for recognition, for her to be "normal" had dissolved like morning mist. In their place grew something I hadn't expected: a deep impulse to share what she had taught me, not as expert to student, but as fellow traveler to fellow traveler.

Enya at Eighteen

The morning I completed the final chapter, Enya sat at our breakfast table with her iPad, playing songs with the focused attention, she had brought to this ritual for years. The same ritual that had anchored her mornings since she was small enough to need a booster seat at that very table.

I watched her methodical movements and felt time folding in on itself. Here was the two-year-old who had first discovered the comfort of routine, the seven-year-old who had taught me about the beauty of repetition, the twelve-year-old who had developed her sophisticated language of signs and sounds and meaningful glances. All of them present in this almost-eighteen-year-old woman who continued to find deep satisfaction in the simple arrangement of songs on YouTube.

She looked up and caught me watching. Her eyes held that familiar directness, but there was something else there now — a settled-ness that hadn't been there even a year earlier. Not resignation, but a kind of comfortable inhabiting of herself that made the approaching number seem both monumentally significant and entirely irrelevant.

"iPad... YouTube," she said, her voice carrying that stretched emphasis that had become her signature way of ensuring important messages were received.

In that simple gesture – taking the iPad, unlocking it, starting YouTube – I felt the weight of all the mornings we had shared. The early ones filled with my anxiety about her development, the middle ones where I had learned to stop timing her routines and start appreciating them, and now this one, where I was beginning to understand that she had been developing exactly as she needed to all along.

The Fierce Advocate

At eighteen, Enya had become the center of a fierce advocacy campaign run by a single dedicated volunteer: her brother. Now nine, Aaryaveer approached her protection with the seriousness of a profession and the creativity of someone who had made it his life's work to ensure the world treated her with appropriate respect.

His latest innovation was what he called "she actually means" – detailed briefings he provided to anyone new who entered her orbit. Teachers, family friends, service providers all received his comprehensive orientation about how to interpret her silence, respect her routines, and recognize her unique forms of communication.

"She's not going to shake your hand," he had informed a relative at a recent family function, his tone suggesting this should be obvious to any reasonable person. "But if she lets you sit next to her while she's doing her things, that means she likes you."

The boy who had once asked "Is she dumb?" had evolved into someone who understood that the question itself revealed the world's confusion, not his sister's limitations. He had learned what took me years to discover: that Enya's differentness wasn't a problem to be solved but a gift to be protected, celebrated, and translated for those not yet wise enough to recognize its value.

The Continuing Journey

The seizures that had introduced such fear into our lives remained controlled through medication. The pills had become simply part of her morning and evening routine, accepted with the same equanimity she brought to everything else. They hadn't diminished the particular quality of awareness that made her who she was – if anything, her personality had become more clearly defined as she had grown into full adulthood.

Just weeks before her eighteenth birthday, she rode her bicycle with the confidence of someone who had mastered balance and momentum. The bicycle mastery had arrived in its own season, meaningful not because of when it happened but because of the integrity with which she approached it.

At eighteen, Enya occupied space in our home with a quiet confidence that had taken years to recognize and appreciate. Her vocabulary remained limited to essential words that served her daily needs: "YouTube" when she wanted music videos, "shoes" when it was time for bicycle rides, "walking" when she needed her evening constitutional. But each word carried weight, used precisely when needed, never wasted on social pleasantries that held no meaning for her.

What struck me most about Enya at eighteen was her contentment. Not the vacant satisfaction that some imagine accompanies cognitive differences, but the deep peace that came from living authentically. She moved through her days guided by internal rhythms that prioritized what brought her genuine pleasure and meaning.

The Goddess in Every Child

During those ten days of Durga Puja when I had finished writing, I watched families stream to temples to honor the divine feminine. Each evening, I returned home to my own goddess – quieter, gentler, but no less powerful in her ability to transform everything she touched.

Every child carries this divine essence. Every child with autism, with ADHD, with any difference that makes the world uncomfortable, carries a piece of what we have forgotten: that being is more important than doing, that presence is more valuable than performance, that love is communicated through a thousand channels beyond words.

My mother's words during a family video call had captured this truth: "Eighteen years ago, I thought I was welcoming a granddaughter who would need taking care of. I didn't realize I was meeting an angel who would take care of all of us."

The Invitation

This book isn't ultimately about autism or special needs parenting. It's about recognizing teachers wherever they appear, receiving wisdom from unexpected sources, and allowing life's challenges to become doorways to forms of consciousness that can't be achieved through effort or acquired through study.

The invitation is to see every person you encounter as a potential teacher, every difficulty as a potential teaching, every moment as an opportunity to practice the forms of awareness that emerge when the wave realizes it was always ocean.

Some of the most profound wisdom comes disguised as limitation. Some of the most important teachings arrive through experiences we would never choose. Some of the greatest teachers speak without words, communicate through presence, and offer their gifts simply by being exactly who they are.

Growing up doesn't have to mean growing away from yourself. Maturity can be the deepening of authenticity rather than the accumulation of social skills. Eighteen years with Enya showed me that the highest intelligence might be the simplest: knowing what you need and creating the conditions for your own flourishing without harming others.

The Wave and the Ocean

Eighteen years had taught me that the ocean was never separate from the waves, that consciousness was never separate from its expressions, that the teacher and student were never two different people. Every wave is equally the ocean. Every person is equally consciousness appearing in temporary form. Every moment is equally an opportunity to remember what we never actually forgot.

As I watched Enya guide my hand to help me with my glasses that final morning of writing – this small gesture carrying more care and intelligence than most conversations I had with speaking adults – I understood that her care-giving, her environmental sensitivity, her capacity for presence weren't compensations for missing abilities. They were expressions of a way of being that most people had forgotten how to access.

The transformation from wave to ocean consciousness isn't a destination to be reached but a recognition to be received. It's available in every moment, with every person, through every experience that life offers – if we can learn to see with the kind of eyes that recognize the extraordinary intelligence operating through even the most ordinary appearances.

The apprenticeship continues. It continued the day she turned eighteen, and it continues now as I share these words.

Because some teachers never stop teaching, and some students never stop learning, and some relationships transcend all categories except love.

Enya never needed to become anything. She needed me to become someone – someone present enough to receive her gifts, humble enough to accept her teaching, wise enough to recognize the divine in disguise.

The eighteenth candle has been lit. And I wait, still learning, still grateful, still amazed by the daughter who arrived as my teacher and will remain so until my final breath.

In gratitude for all the waves that helped this wave remember it was always ocean, and for all the waves yet to come who will continue the endless teaching of what it means to be fully, authentically, compassionately human.

Amar B. Singh

Acknowledgments

This book chronicles my apprenticeship with Enya, but that learning was made possible by an entire ecosystem of people who recognized her worth, supported our family, and created the conditions within which understanding could emerge. Their stories are woven throughout this journey, and their contributions deserve recognition.

To my wife, who walked this path with unwavering dedication when I was still trying to find the way. You bore the daily weight of care while I was learning to see, and your strength created the foundation that allowed our family to not just survive but flourish. This transformation was as much yours as mine.

To my parents, who grieved with us, searched for answers in ways I couldn't always appreciate at the time, and gradually learned to love Enya exactly as she is. Your consultations with astrologers and healers, your prayers and pujas, your relentless hope – all of it contributed to the understanding that some mysteries require multiple lenses to even glimpse their depths.

To my siblings and extended family, who processed this journey in your own ways, offering support that took forms I'm still discovering. Family gatherings became laboratories for acceptance, and through your eyes I learned to see Enya's impact rippling through generations, changing not just parents but grandparents, aunts, uncles, and cousins in ways that continue to unfold.

To the dedicated professionals who became more than service providers – they became partners in recognition. The speech therapists who worked patiently with her silence until they learned to hear what she was communicating through presence. The occupational therapists who helped her engage with the world while teaching us to appreciate her unique ways of processing sensation. The neurologists and doctors who provided medical support while respecting the mystery of consciousness that operates beyond their instruments.

To Action for Autism (AFA), where our formal journey of intervention began. You provided not just therapy services but a community of understanding, a place where different ways of being human were recognized as valid rather than deficient. The foundation you created allowed families like ours to discover that we weren't alone in this territory.

To Prakriti School and Behaviour Momentum India (BMI), whose approaches helped us understand that behavior is always communication, and that our job wasn't to eliminate differences but to decode the intelligence operating through them. You taught us to look beyond surface actions to the needs and capabilities they revealed.

To Soham Foundation and its visionary founder, Mrs. Harshita Sinha, who created not just a school but a sanctuary where Enya's way of being is celebrated rather than corrected. Soham represents everything I dreamed educational environments could become – places organized around recognizing potential rather than measuring deficits, communities where every form of intelligence is valued. Mrs. Sinha, your understanding that different minds require different approaches while maintaining the same respect and expectations has created something revolutionary. Watching Enya flourish in an environment designed around acceptance rather than conformity has been one of the great gifts of this journey.

To the extraordinary community of families at Soham Foundation, who have become our chosen family in ways I never expected. To the other parents who understand the unique challenges and profound gifts that come with loving children who think differently – your friendship has been a source of strength, wisdom, and joy. Together we've created a community that celebrates all festivals, shares all milestones, and supports each other through the challenges that only we truly understand.

Watching our children learn together, play together, and simply be together in an environment of complete acceptance has shown me what inclusive community can look like when it's built on recognition rather than tolerance, celebration rather than accommodation. Our festival gatherings aren't just social events – they're demonstrations of what's possible when diversity is treated as wisdom rather than challenge.

To the teachers, aides, and support staff who have worked with Enya over the years, who learned to communicate in her language rather than insisting she communicate only in theirs. Your patience, creativity, and willingness to see intelligence in unexpected forms made the difference between education that constrains and education that liberates.

To the countless parents I've had the privilege to sit with over the past fifteen years, who shared their own journeys of recognition and taught me that every family's path is unique while the fundamental lessons remain the same. Your courage in facing uncertainty, your commitment to seeing your children's gifts, and your willingness to be changed by the experience of unconditional love have been my teachers as much as Enya has been.

To the friends and colleagues who supported our family through the challenging periods, who celebrated the small victories, and who gradually learned to see Enya through our eyes rather than through the lens of their own assumptions. Your journey from sympathy to recognition, from seeing her as someone to be helped to someone from whom they could learn, mirrors the larger transformation this book chronicles.

To Aaryaveer, my son, Enya's younger brother, who grew up understanding that intelligence comes in many forms, that love doesn't require words, and that some of the most important family members communicate through presence rather than conversation. Watching you two together has taught me more about authentic relationship than any book or theory ever could.

To the broader autism community, both locally and globally, who fight daily for recognition, acceptance, and support for different ways of being human. Your advocacy creates the social conditions within which families like ours can move from surviving to thriving, from hiding differences to celebrating them.

This book is ultimately about an ecosystem of care, understanding, and gradual recognition. None of us made this journey alone. Each person mentioned here, and many others whose contributions I'm still discovering, played essential roles in creating the conditions within which Enya's teachings could be received and this understanding could emerge.

The village that it takes to raise any child becomes even more crucial when that child's gifts operate outside conventional frameworks. You became our village, our community, our chosen family. You saw what we sometimes couldn't see, believed when we struggled to believe, and celebrated every small step toward recognition.

This memoir chronicles my individual journey of learning, but that learning was collective work. Every insight documented here was supported by countless acts of care, understanding, and commitment from people who recognized that Enya's way of being human was worth protecting, nurturing, and celebrating.

To Enya herself, the patient teacher at the center of this story, who waited eighteen years for me to become ready to receive what you've been offering all along. Your gifts to our family, our community, and now to the readers of this book continue to ripple outward in ways we're still discovering. You've taught us that the most profound teachings often come through simply being who you are, and that love expressed through authentic presence is the most powerful force for transformation any of us will ever encounter.

Thank you all for making this journey possible, this understanding available, and this love visible. The apprenticeship continues, and we continue it together.

Glossary

Consciousness & Philosophical Terms

Level 3 Knowledge/Consciousness – Understanding that bypasses analytical thinking and lands directly in the body as lived truth. Distinguished from intellectual knowledge (Level 1) and experiential learning (Level 2). Often arrives suddenly, like "touching a live wire."

Delta Mind – A state of consciousness characterized by deep stillness, presence, and awareness without the need for constant mental activity. Named after the brain's delta waves associated with deep sleep and meditative states.

Enya Circle – The vision of learning communities that approach neurodivergent children as teachers rather than problems to be fixed. Based on the recognition that different ways of being often contain wisdom the typical world needs.

Silent Speech/Language – Communication that occurs without words through presence, gesture, eye contact, body positioning, and energetic awareness. Enya's primary form of expression and connection.

Presence – The quality of being completely here and now, without mental distraction or the need to be elsewhere. A state Enya naturally embodies and teaches others through example.

Autism & Development Terms

Autism Spectrum Disorder (ASD) – A neurological and developmental difference affecting communication, social interaction, and behavior. Increasingly understood as neurodivergence rather than disorder.

Stimming – Self-stimulatory behaviors like rocking, hand-flapping, or repetitive movements that help regulate sensory input and emotional states. Often a sign of engagement rather than distress.

Meltdown – An intense response to overwhelming sensory, emotional, or cognitive input. Different from tantrums, as meltdowns are involuntary and not manipulative.

Theory of Mind – The ability to understand that other people have thoughts, feelings, and perspectives different from one's own. Traditionally seen as challenging for autistic individuals, but may manifest differently rather than being absent.

Masking/Camouflaging – Suppressing natural autistic behaviors and mimicking neurotypical social behaviors. Can be exhausting and lead to loss of authentic self-expression.

Neurodivergent – Having a brain that functions differently from the neurotypical majority. Includes autism, ADHD, dyslexia, and other neurological differences. Viewed as natural human variation rather than pathology.

Special Interests – Intense, focused interests common in autism. Often dismissed as obsessions but may represent deep forms of learning and joy.

Therapeutic & Medical Terms

Speech Therapy – Treatment to improve communication skills, including verbal speech, alternative communication methods, and social communication.

Occupational Therapy – Treatment focusing on daily living skills, sensory processing, fine motor development, and environmental adaptation.

Sensory Processing – How the nervous system receives and responds to sensory information. Many autistic individuals have differences in processing touch, sound, light, movement, and other sensations.

Sensory Diet – A planned set of activities designed to meet an individual's sensory needs throughout the day. May include calming or alerting activities.

Self-Regulation – The ability to manage emotions, behaviors, and attention in response to internal needs and external demands. Develops differently in neurodivergent individuals.

Seizure – Sudden, uncontrolled electrical activity in the brain that can cause changes in behavior, movements, feelings, and consciousness. More common in autistic individuals, especially during adolescence.

Anti-seizure Medication – Drugs used to prevent or reduce the frequency and severity of seizures by stabilizing electrical activity in the brain.

EEG (Electroencephalogram) – A test that measures electrical activity in the brain using electrodes placed on the scalp. Used to diagnose seizure disorders.

Personal & Poetic Terms

The Eighteenth Candle – Symbol of Enya's transition to adulthood and the completion of the author's eighteen-year apprenticeship in learning from her way of being.

Dense Helplessness – The profound powerlessness experienced when a child's medical emergency reveals the limits of parental protection and philosophical understanding.

The Electric Shock – The sudden, physical sensation of Level 3 knowledge arriving, particularly the transformative week when the author first truly *saw* Enya.

Apprenticeship – The author's journey of learning from Enya, positioning himself as student rather than expert in understanding consciousness and authentic being.

The Meltdown Mirror – The recognition that a child's emotional storms often reflect the hidden turbulence in their caregivers.

Repetition as Meditation – Understanding rhythmic, repetitive behaviors not as compulsions to be stopped but as forms of mindfulness practice and self-regulation.

The Half-Closed Eyes – Metaphor for the appearance of disengagement that actually conceals deep, alert awareness. From the poem "Fear Clipped My Wings."

Family Terms

The Protector Reversal – The evolution in sibling relationship from Enya being protected to becoming the protector, then to mutual protection and advocacy.

Silent Conversation – Wordless communication between family members who have learned to read each other's needs, moods, and intentions through presence and attention.

Appendix A: The Three-Level Consciousness Framework

The Odyssey Equation

The framework that emerged from eighteen years with Enya reveals three distinct levels of consciousness that operate when humans encounter circumstances beyond their control. This isn't academic theory but lived discovery, forged through daily experience with challenges that resist conventional solutions.

Level 1: Strategic Consciousness (Delta Mind)

Characteristics:

- Belief that problems can be solved through analysis, effort, and will

- Reality viewed as collection of manageable challenges

- Identity built around competence and control

- Time orientation: future-focused planning and goal achievement

- Response to obstacles: increased effort, more strategies, expert consultation

Applications: Level 1 consciousness works effectively for manageable challenges: career advancement, skill development, logistical problems, technical difficulties. It's the default mode of most adult thinking and the foundation of conventional problem-solving.

Limitations: Becomes counterproductive when applied to mysteries that resist solution: consciousness itself, death, love, meaning, profound human differences. The harder Level 1 tries to control these territories, the more suffering it creates.

In Enya's Story: My first eight years: researching autism therapies, consulting experts, developing comprehensive intervention strategies. Every setback met with renewed determination to find the right combination of treatments.

Level 2: Equanimous Consciousness (Acceptance)

Characteristics:

- Recognition that some things cannot be changed
- Development of equanimity in face of uncontrollable circumstances
- Identity shifts from competence to resilience
- Time orientation: present-moment awareness without urgent future projection
- Response to obstacles: acceptance, adaptation, finding peace within limitations

Applications: Level 2 provides sustainability for long-term challenges: chronic illness, loss, caring for family members with special needs, aging, economic uncertainty. It creates emotional stability and reduces suffering.

Limitations: Can become passive resignation. May miss opportunities for growth or positive change. Sometimes maintains subtle separation between "accepter" and "what must be accepted."

In Enya's Story: Years 8-11: Learning to find peace with her autism, appreciating her unique way of being, stopping the fight against her natural development. This created sustainability but still positioned me as separate from her condition.

Level 3: Unity Consciousness (Recognition)
Characteristics:

- Understanding that separation between observer and observed is conceptual illusion
- Individual identity recognized as temporary wave in infinite ocean
- Time dissolves into eternal present
- Natural compassion arising from recognition of fundamental interconnection
- Response to challenges: no response needed - what appears as problem and problem-solver are one movement

Applications: Level 3 transcends the need for application. It's the recognition that consciousness was never actually divided, that all seeking was the one seeking itself, that every wave was always ocean.

Access Points:

- Deep meditation or contemplative practice
- Profound loss that dissolves identity structures
- Caring for those who embody natural presence
- Any experience that reveals the constructed nature of separation

In Enya's Story: The transformative week when I finally saw her, the seizure experience of dense helplessness, and the gradual recognition that she had never operated from illusion of separation. She was my teacher in what I was trying to achieve.

The Mathematical Expression: Delta + Psi leads to Infinity.

Delta: Represents the strategic mind's attempt to create change through effort

Psi: Represents the acceptance that emerges when effort fails

Infinity: The recognition that the seeker and sought were never separate

The equation suggests that the combination of exhausted effort (Delta) plus developed acceptance (Psi) can open awareness to the infinite - the recognition that individual consciousness was always universal consciousness appearing as individuals.

Practical Applications Beyond Special Needs

Relationships:

- Level 1: Trying to change partner through communication strategies
- Level 2: Accepting partner's unchangeable qualities
- Level 3: Recognizing the one love expressing through apparent two

Career Challenges:

- Level 1: Strategic maneuvering for advancement

- Level 2: Finding contentment within current circumstances
- Level 3: Understanding work as play of consciousness, success and failure as equal expressions

Health Issues:

- Level 1: Aggressive treatment, lifestyle optimization
- Level 2: Peaceful coexistence with chronic conditions
- Level 3: Illness and health as temporary modifications of eternal being

Grief and Loss:

- Level 1: Strategies for "moving through" grief stages
- Level 2: Accepting the ongoing reality of loss
- Level 3: Recognition that what was never born cannot die

Important Distinctions

This is not a hierarchy. Each level serves appropriate functions. Level 1 remains essential for practical matters. Level 2 provides necessary emotional stability. Level 3 isn't an achievement but a recognition available in any moment.

Movement between levels is natural. Most people operate from different levels in different life areas. The framework offers map, not mandate.

Level 3 isn't escape from human experience. It includes but transcends levels 1 and 2. Practical engagement continues, but from understanding rather than compulsion.

Warning Signs of Misunderstanding

Premature Level 3: Using non-dual concepts to avoid Level 1 practical responsibility or Level 2 emotional work

Spiritual Bypassing: Claiming unity consciousness while remaining unconscious of psychological patterns

Conceptual Knowledge: Understanding the framework intellectually without embodied realization

Integration

The framework emerged through lived experience with circumstances that couldn't be controlled, understood, or fixed. It offers orientation for others navigating similar territories - not as technique to master but as recognition to receive.

Enya demonstrated natural Level 3 consciousness throughout her development. She never believed in fundamental separation, never struggled with existential anxiety, never needed to achieve unity she had never lost. She was my teacher in recognizing what had always been true but was obscured by the very effort to find it.

The real odyssey is discovering there was never anywhere to go.

***

Eighteen Years with Enya

Amar B. Singh

Manufactured by Amazon.ca
Acheson, AB